Chef Paul Prudhomme's
Pure Magic

CHEF PAUL PRUDHOMME'S®
MAGIC
Seasoning Blends®

K·PAUL'S
LOUISIANA
·KITCHEN·

L. Paul's Catering Expedition

Good Cooking
Good Eating
Good Loving

ALSO BY CHEF PAUL PRUDHOMME

Chef Paul Prudhomme's Louisiana Kitchen

The Prudhomme Family Cookbook
(WITH THE PRUDHOMME FAMILY)

Chef Paul Prudhomme's Seasoned America

Chef Paul Prudhomme's Fork in the Road

Chef Paul
Prudhomme's
Pure Magic

PHOTOGRAPHS BY
PAUL RICO

WILLIAM MORROW AND COMPANY, INC.
NEW YORK

Library of Congress Cataloging-in-Publication Data

Prudhomme, Paul.
Chef Paul Prudhomme's pure magic / photographs by Paul Rico.
p.   cm.
Includes index.
ISBN 0-688-14202-8
1. Cookery (Herbs)   2. Spices.   3. Cookery, American—Louisiana style.
I. Title.   II. Title: Pure magic.
TX819.H4P778   1995
641.6'57—dc20   94-46213
CIP

Printed in the United States of America
First Edition
8 9 10

BOOK DESIGN BY DEBORAH KERNER

This book is dedicated to three very special people, each of whom left us during 1994. Their wisdom, kindness, and generosity have been an important part of my life, and I will always treasure their memory.

To LOU HINRICHS,
who has joined his precious daughter, K, my late wife and partner, in the hereafter.

To my brother BOBBY,
who was closest to me in age and just as close to my heart. He was my constant friend and companion in childhood and a trusted and invaluable adviser throughout our lives together. He devoted many years to helping me succeed, especially as the keeper of my Magic Seasoning Blends formulas and the family recipes for tasso and andouille.

To LYMAN BARSTOW MCBRIDE,
whom I came to know and respect for his love of life, his caring for others, his infectious enthusiasm, and his keen appreciation of the joys of life. He was a true gentleman who understood the importance of personal style, self-reliance, and generosity. I am saddened by his leaving, but I am pleased to see that these fine qualities have been passed on to his son, John McBride, and his grandson, Brendan.

★

A Message from the President of Magic Seasoning Blends

Chef Paul Prudhomme has influenced the way people eat all over the world. The impact of his talent in the kitchen has been felt on restaurant menus and family tables everywhere. Chef Paul has always loved to share his knowledge of food, and he has dedicated his life to making your food taste better.

For many years Chef Paul has labored to make his recipes accessible to any interested cook. We have distributed millions of recipes through television and radio appearances, magazines, newspapers, grocery stores, mail-order catalogs, food expos, telephones, and fax machines, not to mention his four best-selling cookbooks, *Chef Paul Prudhomme's Louisiana Kitchen, Family Cookbook, Seasoned America,* and *Fork in the Road.*

Pure Magic combines the great taste of Chef Paul's most requested recipes with the convenience of his Magic Seasoning Blends. Every recipe was either created using Magic Seasoning Blends or converted and retested by Chef Paul especially for this book. Some of these recipes originated in Chef Paul's other books. Some came from K-Paul's Louisiana Kitchen Restaurant, and others were requested by Magic Seasoning Blends for specific projects. Still others were created by Chef Paul for special events and have never been printed before.

Whether the recipes are old or new, Magic Seasoning Blends make them uniformly delicious and even quicker and easier to prepare. Don't stop with the Magic in this book—let Magic Seasoning Blends transform all your favorite recipes.

Acknowledgments

For every book written, there are always a number of people who quietly devote a part of their lives to making it a reality. I can assure you that the tasks of testing, retesting, and recipe perfecting are not easy ones. Truly useful recipes require a great deal of careful thought, and the effort requires a committed team.

Not only has Patricia Kennedy Livingston been tireless throughout the huge task of testing, editing, retesting, and writing, but she has also been a very patient and understanding friend. Despite my impossible travel schedule, which kept her working at all sorts of odd hours, she somehow managed to keep everything moving forward at a very fast clip. I still look over my shoulder late at night or in the early morning, half expecting to see Patricia with an armful of samples to be tasted. Thank you, Patricia, for being so patient and so persistent.

Sean O'Meara, our resident computer genius and food lover, not only kept the computers in fighting trim but also assisted mightily in the testing of recipes and in the editing process.

And "Madame President," Shawn Granger McBride, kept us all going on those eighteen-hour days with her sense of humor, endless energy, and unwavering commitment to do the manuscript over and over until it was done right. When our energy started to fade and our feet began to falter, Shawn would be there with her favorite words of wisdom: "Come on, guys! Let's get back to work!"

Special thanks are owed to John McBride, Dudley Passman, and Marty Cosgrove, who head up the sales and marketing teams at Magic Seasoning Blends. It was their initial groundwork that was the force behind this book, and their hard work was invaluable throughout the process, helping us with selection, editing, revising, and the many other tasks that needed to be done. I am very fortunate to be working with such true professionals. Their work makes mine possible.

Two other people at Magic Seasoning Blends also deserve special thanks: Paula Messina LaCour, our controller, who never fails to keep us in line and under budget and is always ready to lend a hand wherever it is needed, and Margie Noonan Blaum, my indispensable right hand and resident gentle spirit.

To William Morrow and Company, our publishers, and especially president Allen Marchioni and our wonderful editor, Ann Bramson, there are truly no words to express our appreciation. But if there were, Ann could certainly find them. I have heard horror stories from some of my friends who have written books for other publishers, so I feel doubly blessed that our relationship has been both productive and enjoyable.

Special thanks also go to Paul Rico, not only for his superb photography, but for undertaking this work on very short notice. Somehow he managed to squeeze four days of work into two without sacrificing either his professionalism or his sense of humor. Paul's artistry is a delight to watch, and his results are so beautiful that I am tempted to nibble at the negatives.

Finally, and most importantly, thanks are also in order for my many friends, supporters, and customers. To the many people who have become Magic Seasoning Blend users and to the loyal customers who visit my restaurant year after year, let me say "Thank you" as loud as I can. Your loyalty to me and to my products has been my greatest reward over the years. Whenever you see me on TV or at a demonstration or cooking for charity, remember that I am there only because of your support. You are very much a part of what I do, and since I cannot thank each of you personally, I give you my promise and commitment: I will make sure that all of my products will always be the very best that I know how to make.

Contents

Author's Preface

Let me tell you how Magic Seasoning Blends were born.

I grew up on a farm, the youngest of thirteen children. Mom was a great cook, skilled at using all the wonderful fresh ingredients that south Louisiana had to offer, along with herbs and spices to season them. I grew up surrounded by the unbelievable aromas of green coffee being roasted, flour being browned, and fresh fish being fried. I have happy memories of boiling crawfish in a huge iron kettle with the entire family gathered around, all of us rejoicing in the fantastic spicy fragrance and our anticipation of how great the meal was going to be.

I remember how good all of our food tasted, and how emotional we were about it—we'd take a bite and just couldn't resist telling everyone within shouting distance how wonderful it was. I simply assumed that everyone had food as exciting as ours and that they got as steamed up about it as we did. So when I traveled across the country to learn about food in other places, I was really surprised that the level of excitement I had experienced all my life just didn't exist elsewhere. There was a lot of good food out there, but people didn't have the same level of emotional involvement.

When I cooked for people in other parts of the country, I was glad to see that they reacted with enthusiasm to the kinds of seasonings I used. For instance, during the time I worked at a really fine Italian restaurant in Denver, I would secretly bring in herbs from outside to add to their recipes. I'd have oregano in one pocket, basil in another, and so on. I got tired of trying to remember what was in which pocket, so I started mixing the blends at home. They worked pretty well, but I was always afraid someone might catch me. Management might not have approved of what I was doing—after all, I was messing with their recipes—but patrons raved about all the dishes that came from my station.

When I returned to Louisiana, I didn't immediately put that discovery to use because my first project was to record and save traditional recipes of the region that were in danger of being lost. Families—including mine—were changing their ways of cooking and not passing on their knowledge to younger generations. My wife, K, and I started our restaurant, K-Paul's Louisiana Kitchen, and I published *Chef Paul Prudhomme's Louisiana Kitchen* cookbook, both to help document this kind of cooking and to give pleasure to people who got as excited about our food as we did.

Customers often would ask what kind of seasoning we used for this dish or that one, and for a while we simply explained that we used a balance of herbs and spices and gave them little samples. After a while, though, people seemed embarrassed to ask repeatedly for free samples, so in 1983 we started mixing up batches and putting them in plastic zip bags to sell.

Well, the blends became so popular that soon we couldn't keep up with demand, so our next step was to mix up larger amounts and package them in bottles. We worked on weekends, when restaurant employees wanted to earn a little extra income, but we still had problems. I remember how hard it was to get the labels to stick to the bottles, and no one wanted the job of wetting the glue on the label. You wouldn't believe how excited we all were when we got our first glue machine—a simple thing with rollers and a reservoir for the glue—which could label maybe five bottles a minute. We thought we were Big Business! Our first salesman sold our products out of the trunk of his car, but before very long, we had so much business that his trunk was too small. So we bought a truck and I learned a wonderful new word: "distributor." With help from our new business contacts, we started placing our Magic Seasoning Blends in local supermarkets, then regional ones. Before we knew it, our distribution network stretched all the way across the country. Since that time I have been privileged to make friends and meet wonderful people almost everywhere in the U.S. and around the globe. And all the while we have grown and grown. Our Magic Seasoning Blends family of employees still has many original members—most have been with us almost a decade. We truly have grown together. Today our automated production line handles more than one hundred units a minute, and our blends are available literally all over the world.

Magic Seasoning Blends work well with all types of cuisines—everything from Italian to Mexican to French to Chinese—or wherever good food is appreciated. Our products are all natural and contain no preservatives or MSG. You can substitute them in all of your everyday recipes by simply eliminating the herbs, spices, salt, and pepper called for and substituting approximately two-thirds of the amount of Magic Seasoning Blends. Or simply sprinkle it on your fish, vegetables, meat, eggs, etc., before you begin your cooking process.

I sincerely hope you enjoy using Magic Seasoning Blends and that this new book will add to your cooking and eating pleasure.

Good Cooking!
Good Eating!
Good Loving!

Notes from
Our Kitchen to Yours

Throughout this book you'll see references to this section in regard to stock, chile peppers, browning flour, and so forth. After you've tried one or two of the recipes, you'll remember these notes and won't need to refer to them. But in the meantime I'd like to share a few of my secrets with you.

STOCK

With very few exceptions, we cook these dishes with stock rather than water. Now, I have nothing against water—it's great for washing, swimming, and floating boats—but in cooking, water takes away most of the taste developed by the cooking methods in this book, whereas stock adds flavor. There's really nothing to it. Just remember to start your stock as you begin the recipe. Even better, if you have time, start it early so it can simmer for several hours, but stock that's cooked for only 30 minutes is still better than water. And there are one or two recipes that require stock but have few ingredients to prepare, and for them you'll need to start your stock early to have it ready in time.

Start with 2 quarts of *cold* water and add the trimmings from the vegetables in the recipe you're making or from vegetables you have on hand—an excellent way to use scraps that would otherwise be thrown away. Experienced cooks often make stock with kitchen scraps even if they have no immediate use for it. If you don't have vegetable trimmings, use an unpeeled, quartered onion, an unpeeled, quartered large garlic clove, and a rib of celery. (The peelings add flavor, and quartering the vegetables opens them up to release even more flavor.) If you're making vegetable stock, just bring to a boil, reduce the heat, and simmer for as long as possible. Add water only if the level drops below 1 quart.

If you're making meat or poultry stock, add the bones and excess meat (including giblets, other than liver, from the bird), and if you're making seafood stock, use the shells and carcasses. Never add spices or bell peppers. Stock freezes well, and if you reduce it first by simmering over low heat, it will be even more flavorful and take up less space in the freezer.

For a richer taste, first roast the bones for 30 minutes in a 350° oven. To defat stock, refrigerate it overnight, then remove the fat that rises to the top and congeals. Pour the *very cold* stock in a thin stream over ice packed in a strainer placed over a container large enough to hold it. The extra chilling provided by the ice traps any fats remaining in the stock. For complete stock recipes, see pages 194–198.

PEPPERS

Many of these dishes call for ground dried chile peppers. If you can't find ready-ground peppers, buy whole dried ones and grind them yourself. A coffee grinder works really well and is inexpensive, or you can use a food processor. If the peppers aren't brittle enough for grinding, first roast them in a 200° oven for about 10 minutes, or until crisp. Overroasting may create a dark, bitter taste. Cool for a few minutes, remove the seeds (or leave the seeds in place if you prefer a little more heat), then process.

Some of the varieties I like to use and can easily find in New Orleans supermarkets are New Mexico, ancho, guajillo, arbol, habañero and pasilla. Experiment with the chiles you find where you shop—they will vary in heat—and you will notice that using a combination of varieties gives you a round, well-balanced flavor. Use whatever chiles are available but don't use commercial chili powder, which contains other seasonings. Chiles vary considerably in heat level, so always taste before grinding and mixing and use your good judgment. If possible, use brands of chiles that have a heat rating on the package.

ANDOUILLE AND TASSO

Made in the Acadian country of southwest Louisiana, andouille and tasso are highly seasoned smoked pork sausage and ham. Some meat processors use turkey to produce a low-fat version. If you can't find andouille and tasso, you can use any top-quality smoked sausage and ham. The dense meat from smoked turkey wings also works well in place of tasso. A word of caution: True andouille and tasso are very spicy, so taste your dish carefully as you season to avoid overdoing it.

BROWNING FLOUR

Preheat a small nonstick skillet over high heat for 3 minutes. Add the specified amount of flour and whisk to break up the lumps. When the flour starts to brown, reduce the heat to low, and stir constantly. *Caution: After about 4 or 5 minutes, the flour will burn easily.* As soon as the flour is a milk-chocolate brown color (about 6 minutes), turn off the heat, sift the flour, and set it aside until needed in the recipe.

PEELING TOMATOES

To make tomato skins come off easily, first score the skins with an "X" on the flower end, then drop the whole tomatoes into boiling water for a minute or so. Remove them with a slotted spoon and place in ice water in a bowl large enough to hold all the tomatoes. The skins should slip right off while the meat remains firm.

SCALLOPING MEAT

Place the meat on a firm surface in front of you. With a very sharp heavy knife held almost parallel to the meat, slice through the meat about ¼ inch below the surface at about a 30-degree angle from the meat's grain, and cut off a piece about 2 by 3 inches. Think of the scallop as a slice of potato for scalloped potatoes—it's thin and more or less oval. That's the shape you're trying for.

Make the next cut right next to the first, also at about a 30-degree angle from the meat's grain, but in the opposite direction. Continue down the length of the piece of meat, then through the thickness. You are removing thin ovals from the top of the meat from one end to the other, making the meat thinner with each successive layer of cuts. Don't hurry the process, and try to keep the scallops as nearly the same size as possible so they will all cook in about the same amount of time.

JULIENNE

The term *julienne* refers to food—meat or vegetables—cut into long, thin strips about ¼ inch by 2 to 2½ inches. "Matchstick" vegetables, not used in this book, would be cut even smaller. The sharper the knife, the easier it is to produce julienne cuts.

SUBSTITUTING MAGIC SEASONING BLENDS

To substitute Magic Seasoning Blends for the seasoning mixes called for in my other cookbooks, simply add up the quantities listed for dried herbs and spices and use about two-thirds of that amount of the appropriate Magic Seasoning. For instance, if you're cooking a chicken dish, you'll use Poultry Magic, and if you making a beef recipe, you'll use Meat Magic. Don't be compulsive about this, though—use whatever seasoning blend you prefer on whatever you're cooking. We don't have a Magic Seasoning Blends Patrol to make sure you're using the blends strictly according to the labels!

I hope you will taste your dishes as you cook them because only you can determine exactly how much seasoning to use for the result you want. If the taste seems a little flat, add more salt, not more seasoning. Remember, Magic Seasoning Blends are lower in salt than most blends—some are almost completely salt-free. If you generally prefer your food less highly seasoned than the average, use a little less of the Magic Seasoning Blends than the two-thirds suggested here, or if you like more seasoning, just add it to the recipe.

If the recipe includes sweet spices (such as allspice, cardamom, cinnamon, cloves, or nutmeg) or any truly distinctive seasonings (such as curry powder,

Oriental or Thai seasonings, or chile peppers), then add them in the amount called for and determine the amount of Magic Seasoning Blends to use by totaling the other dried herbs and spices.

"IN ALL"

You'll notice the phrase "in all" after many of the ingredients, such as "1½ cups chopped onions, *in all*." We use this phrase when the ingredient is not used at one time in the recipe. One of the secrets I learned from helping my mother cook was that certain vegetables, such as onions, bell peppers, and celery, change their flavors dramatically as they are browned. The flavor of a dish is built up and becomes more complex when these ingredients are added at different stages in the cooking.

Sometimes other kinds of ingredients, such as butter, milk, or stock, are added at different times, so we use "in all" in those instances as well. It just means that you don't add all of the ingredient at once.

BUILDING FLAVORS

If it were possible to put all the ingredients in the pot at the same time and come up with a great dish, everyone would be a fantastic cook. But in my recipes, you'll notice that I add ingredients in stages, instead of all at once. The first 5 to 10 minutes of cooking are the most important period, because that is when the distinctive flavors begin to develop.

The flavor of the ingredients is developed as their surface moisture evaporates over the high, dry heat, changing the fibers' natural flavors within. As the ingredients are added, they develop their own special flavors—some cooking longer than others. Even when I add a liquid like stock, I add it in stages and allow it to evaporate so that the other ingredients cook and change flavor.

Soup's On

Beef Vegetable Soup

MAKES **6** MAIN-DISH SERVINGS

Nothing fixes whatever's wrong like a big steaming pot of homemade soup! And when you grow up on a farm, as I did, you get a lot of vegetable soup, made even more delicious by a big, meaty bone. If you want to serve your soup the way we do in Louisiana, place a heaping tablespoon of cooked rice in the bowl first.

2 quarts beef stock (see page 198)

2 pounds bone-in beef soup meat, about 1 inch thick, cut into 4 to 6 pieces

1 pound bone-in chuck roast, cut into 1-inch cubes

1 cup chopped onions

1 cup peeled and chopped tomatoes

½ cup chopped celery

½ cup medium-diced carrots

½ cup canned tomato sauce

¼ cup chopped green bell peppers

2 tablespoons **Chef Paul Prudhomme's Meat Magic**

¾ pound medium-diced turnips

1 cup medium-diced peeled potatoes

1 cup chopped cabbage

½ cup uncooked twist macaroni (preferably rotini)

6 string beans, trimmed and sliced into 1-inch pieces

¼ cup peas, fresh (preferred) or frozen

¼ cup chopped green onion tops

Combine the stock, meat, and bones in a 6-quart pot over high heat. Bring to a boil, reduce the heat, cover, and simmer, stirring occasionally, for 45 minutes. Return the heat to high and stir in the onions, tomatoes, celery, carrots, tomato sauce, bell peppers, and Meat Magic. When the soup comes

continued

just to a boil again, reduce the heat and simmer, uncovered, stirring occasionally, for 30 minutes.

Stir in the turnips, potatoes, cabbage, macaroni, beans, and peas. When the soup comes to a boil again, reduce the heat and simmer, stirring occasionally, until the vegetables are tender but still firm, about 30 minutes. Skim any fat from the surface as it appears. Stir in the green onions, cook for 5 minutes more, and remove from the heat. Skim off any visible fat before serving.

★

Cream of Tomato Soup

MAKES ABOUT 10 CUPS, ENOUGH FOR 10 TO 12 FIRST-COURSE SERVINGS

Selecting the tomatoes is the most important part of this dish. Avoid the mounds of supermarket tomatoes, all the same size and color. Dangerous! Dangerous! Tasteless! Even if you don't have a gardening neighbor, you can often find vine-ripened tomatoes in the store, or look for the ones that are all different shapes and colors. Unripened tomatoes should be kept in a sunny window until they ripen.

SEASONING MIX

2 tablespoons *Chef Paul*
  Prudhomme's Seafood Magic
1 tablespoon sugar
½ teaspoon ground nutmeg

•

1 cup heavy cream
4 tablespoons unsalted butter

1½ cups chopped onions
½ cup chopped celery
11 cups peeled (see page 3) and
  chopped very ripe tomatoes,
  about 16 (see Note)
1½ cups chicken stock
  (see page 196)
¼ cup chopped fresh parsley

Combine the seasoning mix ingredients in a small bowl.

Bring the cream just to the boiling point in a small saucepan. Remove from the heat and set aside.

Melt the butter in a heavy 3-quart pot (do *not* use cast-iron) over high heat. Add the onions and celery and cook, stirring occasionally, for 12 minutes. Stir in *2 tablespoons* of the seasoning mix and cook for 2 minutes. Stir in the tomatoes and the remaining seasoning mix, cover, and bring to a rolling boil. Uncover, stir well, and cook hard for about 3 minutes. Stir in the stock and bring to a boil. Cover, reduce the heat to low, and simmer for 10 minutes. Uncover, raise the heat to high, and cook for 10 minutes more. Stir in the parsley and remove from the heat.

Put the soup into a food processor in 2 batches and process until coarsely puréed but not quite smooth. Pour into a large bowl and stir in the reserved warm cream.

NOTE: You can use any variety, including Italian plum tomatoes, adjusting the number as necessary to get 11 cups chopped tomatoes.

Corn Chowder

MAKES 10 TO 12 SERVINGS

★ ★ ☆ ★ ★ ★ ☆ ★

This perennial American favorite is creamy and filling, just perfect for the crisp days of autumn. Because our version is cooked less than 30 minutes after the corn is added, the flavor of the fresh corn really comes across. I think this soup goes great with crusty dark bread and a green salad. Be sure to select the freshest corn you can. The way to tell the freshness of corn is by pressing your thumbnail into one kernel. The liquid should squirt out.

SEASONING MIX
4 tablespoons **Chef Paul Prudhomme's Vegetable Magic**
1 teaspoon dried thyme leaves
¾ teaspoon dried marjoram leaves

•

6 slices bacon, diced
1 cup chopped celery
3 cups chopped onions, in all

1 medium-large potato, peeled and grated
6 cups chicken stock, in all (see page 196)
7 cups fresh corn kernels (about 14 ears)
2 cups finely diced peeled potatoes
1 tablespoon dark brown sugar, optional
1 cup heavy cream

Combine the seasoning mix ingredients in a small bowl.

Place the bacon in a heavy 5-quart pot over high heat. Cover and cook, stirring occasionally, until crisp, about 5 to 6 minutes. Remove the bacon with a slotted spoon and drain it on paper towels.

Add the celery, *2 cups* of the onions, and the seasoning mix to the pot. Cover and cook, scraping the bottom once or twice, until the onions are golden, about 4 to 5 minutes. Spread the grated potato over the onions, cover, and cook for 2 minutes, then mix the potato with the rest of the ingredients. Cover and cook just until the mixture starts to brown and stick to the bottom of the pot, about 5 minutes. Add *2 cups* of the stock, scrape the bottom of the pot, cover, and cook for 1 minute. By now you should have a rich, light brown mixture that is wonderfully fragrant. Add *1 more cup* of stock and scrape the bottom clean again. Cover and bring to a rolling boil.

Reduce the heat to medium and cook, stirring occasionally, for 2 minutes. Break up the potato with a whisk and blend it into the stock. Return the heat to high and add the corn, remaining onions and remaining 3 cups of stock. Scrape the bottom of the pot and bring to a boil. Cover and cook, stirring occasionally, for 8 minutes. Whisk the mixture thoroughly and cook, stirring occasionally, for 6 minutes. Add the diced potatoes, stir, and cook for 8 to 10 minutes more. If you wish to add the sugar, do so now. Stir in the cream and bring to a boil, reduce the heat, and simmer for 3 minutes. Remove from the heat and stir the bacon into the soup.

SEE COLOR PHOTOGRAPH

Milwaukee Potato Soup

If you think potato soup is bland, have we got a happy surprise for you! This recipe truly lets you taste starches cooked for different lengths of time, and the herbs and spices lift those individual flavors to a warm, cuddly, starch ecstasy. I like to serve this with plenty of homemade toasted bread or muffins and a salad of oranges and red onions.

SEASONING MIX
5 tablespoons **Chef Paul Prudhomme's Vegetable Magic**
2 tablespoons **Chef Paul Prudhomme's Poultry Magic**
½ teaspoon ground cinnamon
½ teaspoon ground nutmeg

•

7 large potatoes
12 tablespoons (1½ sticks) unsalted butter, in all

1 cup grated onions (grated through the large holes of a hand grater)
1 cup chopped celery
5 cups chicken stock, in all (see page 196)
6 cups milk
2 cups sliced onions, each slice cut in half
1 cup heavy cream

Combine the seasoning mix ingredients in a small bowl.

Peel the potatoes. Cut 3 of them into small dice, and 2 into medium dice, which will make about 8 cups of diced potatoes in all. Grate the other 2 potatoes through the large holes of a hand grater; this should make about 3 cups.

Place a large, heavy pot over high heat and add *1 stick* of the butter. When it starts to sizzle, add the grated potatoes, grated onions, celery, and seasoning mix. Cover and cook, scraping the bottom of the pot occasionally, until the mixture starts to stick hard, about 8 to 10 minutes. Be careful not to let the mixture get dark brown or the soup will be too dark. Add *1 cup* of the stock and scrape up the crust on the bottom of the pot—the mixture will look somewhat pasty. Add *3 more cups* of stock, scrape the bottom of the pot, and bring to a rolling boil. Stir in the milk and the remaining cup of stock, bring just to a simmer, reduce the heat, and simmer for 5 minutes. Once you add milk, do not bring the mixture to a hard boil or the liquid is likely to "break," or separate.

Add the diced potatoes, cover, and cook for 5 minutes. Add the sliced onions, cover, and cook, scraping the bottom of the pot from time to time, for about 15 minutes. Reduce the heat, cover, and simmer, occasionally scraping the bottom of the pot, for 20 minutes. Uncover and simmer, scraping and whisking from time to time, for 15 minutes.

Cut the remaining 4 tablespoons (½ stick) of butter into pats, add them to the soup along with the cream, and whisk until the butter is thoroughly blended, about 6 minutes. Remove from the heat and serve immediately.

SEE COLOR PHOTOGRAPH

Black Bean Soup

MAKES 10 SERVINGS

Beans are versatile and nutritious, and we've spiced them up with an exciting blend of ground chile peppers. Don't be afraid of the peppers, because if you prefer less heat, you can always use a smaller amount. If you can't find these same varieties where you shop, use what are available, but do use several kinds of varying heats for a rounded taste. And see page 2 for more information on chile peppers and how to prepare them.

1 pound dried black beans

SEASONING MIX
*3 tablespoons plus 1 teaspoon **Chef Paul Prudhomme's Poultry Magic***
1 tablespoon ground dried ancho chile pepper (see page 2)
2 teaspoons ground dried guajillo chile pepper (see page 2)
2 teaspoons ground dried pasilla chile pepper (see page 2)
2 teaspoons ground dried New Mexico chile pepper (see page 2)

1 teaspoon crushed red pepper flakes
1 teaspoon ground nutmeg

•

¼ cup yellow cornmeal
½ pound bacon, diced
4 cups chopped onions, in all
1 cup chopped celery
6 cups chicken stock, in all (see page 196)
2 cups chopped green bell peppers
1 tablespoon minced fresh garlic
¼ cup chopped fresh cilantro

DAY 1 • Add enough water to the beans to cover them by 3 or 4 inches, and soak overnight in the refrigerator.

DAY 2 • Combine the seasoning mix ingredients in a small bowl.

Toast the cornmeal in a small skillet over medium heat, stirring and shaking the pan frequently, until lightly toasted, about 3 to 5 minutes. Remove from the heat and set aside.

Drain the beans.

Fry the bacon in a large heavy pot (cast-iron is best) over high heat, stirring occasionally, until golden brown, about 7 to 9 minutes. Stir in *2 cups* of the onions, all the celery, and *3 tablespoons* of the seasoning mix; cover and cook for 3 minutes. Stir in *1 cup* of the stock and scrape up the crust on the bottom of the pot. Add the beans, cover, and cook, occasionally scraping the bottom of the pot, for about 18 minutes. Add *2 cups* more stock, scrape the pot bottom clean, and cook, stirring occasionally, for 3 minutes. Add *2 cups* more stock, *2 tablespoons* of the seasoning mix, the bell peppers, garlic, and the remaining 2 cups of onions. Cover and bring to a boil. Reduce the heat to low and simmer, stirring occasionally, for about 27 minutes.

Stir in the remaining 1 cup stock and the remaining seasoning mix, cover, and simmer for 45 minutes. Stir in the toasted cornmeal and the cilantro. Cover and cook until the beans are tender, about 15 minutes.

Serve garnished with thin lemon slices or a dollop of sour cream if desired.

SEE COLOR PHOTOGRAPH

Totally
Veggie Vegetarian Soup

This hearty soup is full of flavor, is extremely low in calories, and has absolutely no fat! You'll notice that I've listed three of my seasonings—take your choice, because each one is different and each one is great.

10 cups vegetable stock, in all
  (see page 195)

3 tablespoons **Chef Paul
  Prudhomme's Vegetable Magic**
  (preferred), or 2 tablespoons plus
  1 teaspoon **Chef Paul
  Prudhomme's Meat Magic**, or
  3 tablespoons **Chef Paul
  Prudhomme's Poultry Magic**

1 large onion, peeled and cut into
  8 to 10 wedges, in all

1 large potato, peeled, cut into 1-
  inch rounds, and quartered, in all

2 large carrots, scrubbed, cut
  lengthwise in half, then into
  1-inch pieces, in all

½ small green cabbage, cut into
  4 or 5 wedges, in all

1 large red bell pepper, cut into
  1-inch pieces, in all

1 large yellow bell pepper, cut into
  1-inch pieces, in all

1 medium-size turnip, scrubbed and
  cut into 10 wedges, in all

1 medium-size rutabaga, peeled
  and cut into 10 wedges, in all

4 ribs bok choy, cut into 1-inch
  diagonal pieces, in all

2 cups apple juice

Place a heavy 10-quart pot over high heat and add *6 cups* of the stock. Bring to a full boil, then add the Vegetable Magic (or other Magic Seasoning Blend) and *one fourth* of each vegetable. Cook until the vegetables are tender, about 14 to 16 minutes. Strain the cooked vegetables, reserving the broth, and transfer them to a food processor. Purée the vegetables, adding a little of the reserved broth if necessary, until they are liquefied, about 2 to 3 minutes.

Return the puréed mixture to the pot, adding the remaining 4 cups of stock and the apple juice, mix together, and bring to a boil. Add the remaining vegetables and return the mixture to a boil over high heat. Reduce the heat to medium, cover, and simmer until the vegetables are fork tender, about 25 to 30 minutes.

Green Chili

☆☆☆☆☆☆

This green-hot chili packs a wallop, but if you have a wimpy guest like my friend Mrs. Podunk, you can serve plenty of tortillas and some cool guacamole. The chili gets its color from the combination of fresh green peppers—sweet bell peppers and hot chile peppers.

3 tablespoons **Chef Paul
  Prudhomme's Meat Magic,**
  in all
1 tablespoon ground cumin, in all
⅜ teaspoon ground nutmeg, in all
1½ pounds ground pork
½ cup pork lard or chicken fat
  (either preferred) or vegetable oil
1½ (6-inch) corn tortillas
1 teaspoon dried oregano leaves
2½ cups chopped onions, in all

2 cups chopped green bell peppers,
  in all
1¼ cups canned diced green chile
  peppers and their juice, in all
¼ cup minced fresh jalapeño
  peppers, in all
1½ teaspoons minced garlic
⅓ cup all-purpose flour
5 cups pork or chicken stock, in all
  (see page 198 or 196)

Combine *1 tablespoon plus 1 teaspoon* of the Meat Magic, *½ teaspoon* of the cumin, and *⅛ teaspoon* of the nutmeg. Sprinkle the pork evenly with this mixture and mix by hand until thoroughly combined.

Melt the lard or chicken fat (or heat the oil) in a heavy 4-quart pot over high heat. Add the meat and, stirring as necessary, cook just until browned. Remove the meat with a slotted spoon, getting as many of the tiny pieces out as possible, and set aside.

In the same oil, fry the tortillas over high heat until browned and very crisp, then drain on paper towels.

Combine the remaining Meat Magic, cumin, nutmeg, and the oregano in a small bowl, then add to the hot oil. Cook the seasonings over high heat, stirring constantly, until they roast, about 10 to 15 seconds. Add *1½ cups* of the onions and cook, stirring constantly and scraping the pan bottom well, for 10 to 15 seconds. Stir in *1 cup* of the bell peppers, *½ cup* of the green chiles, and *2 tablespoons* of the jalapeño peppers. Cook for 8 minutes, stirring fairly often—constantly toward the end of cooking time—and scraping the pan bottom well each time. Stir in the garlic and cook and stir a few seconds. Add the flour, stirring until well blended and scraping the pan bottom clean, and cook for 2 to 3 minutes, stirring and scraping almost constantly to make sure the mixture doesn't scorch. (Soups containing ground meat and flour stick more than other types of soup.)

Add *1 cup* of the stock, scraping the pan bottom until all the browned bits are dissolved, then add the remaining 4 cups of stock. Stir until well blended and scrape the pan bottom clean again. Continue cooking over high heat, stirring occasionally.

Meanwhile, remove 1 cup of the stock from this mixture and place in a food processor. Crumble the fried tortillas, add them to the processor, and process until the tortillas are finely chopped, about 30 to 45 seconds. Stir the tortilla mixture into the cooking stock mixture. Stir in the remaining onions and bell peppers, then add the meat, stirring well. Bring the mixture to a boil, stirring occasionally, then reduce the heat and simmer, stirring and scraping fairly often (be careful not to let the mixture scorch) for 50 minutes. Stir in the remaining green chiles and jalapeño peppers, and simmer and stir for 15 minutes. Skim off any oil from the surface and serve immediately.

Seafood Gumbo
with Smoked Sausage

Gumbo is probably south Louisiana's best culinary gift to the rest of the country, and seafood/sausage is probably the most popular type of gumbo. This one is fragrant and rich with savory vegetables and spices, yet so easy to prepare that even a beginning cook can master it.

2 cups chopped onions, in all
1½ cups chopped green bell
  peppers, in all
1 cup chopped celery, in all
¾ cup vegetable oil
¾ cup all-purpose flour
1 tablespoon plus 2 teaspoons **Chef Paul Prudhomme's Seafood Magic**, or 1 tablespoon plus 1 teaspoon **Chef Paul Prudhomme's Blackened Redfish Magic**, or 1 tablespoon **Chef Paul Prudhomme's Meat Magic** plus 1 tablespoon **Chef Paul Prudhomme's Poultry Magic**

1 tablespoon minced fresh garlic
5½ cups seafood stock
  (see page 194)
1 pound andouille (preferred) or
  top-quality smoked pork sausage,
  cut into ½-inch pieces
1 pound peeled medium shrimp
1 dozen shucked medium to large
  oysters in their liquor (the liquid
  in which they're packed), about
  9 ounces
¾ pound crabmeat, picked over for
  shell and cartilage
2½ cups hot cooked white rice

Combine the onions, bell peppers, and celery in a bowl and set aside.

Make a roux by heating the oil in a large, heavy skillet over high heat until it begins to smoke, about 5 minutes, then gradually whisking in the flour. Continue cooking, whisking constantly, until the roux is dark red-brown, about 2 to 4 minutes, but be careful not to let it scorch or splash on your skin. Immediately add *half* the vegetables and stir well (switch to a spoon if necessary). Continue stirring and cooking for 1 minute, then add the remaining vegetables and cook and stir for 2 minutes. Stir in the Seafood Magic (or other Magic Seasoning) and continue cooking, stirring frequently, for 2 minutes. Add the garlic, stir well, then cook and stir for 1 minute more. Remove from the heat.

Bring the stock to a boil in a 5½-quart pot or Dutch oven over high heat. Add the roux mixture by spoonfuls to the boiling stock, stirring until dissolved between each addition. Bring the mixture to a boil, add the andouille, and return to a boil. Continue boiling, stirring occasionally, for 15 minutes. Reduce the heat to low and simmer for 10 minutes. Add the shrimp, undrained oysters, and crabmeat. Return to a boil over high heat, stirring occasionally. Remove from the heat and skim off any oil that appears on the surface. Serve immediately.

To serve as a main course, mound ¼ cup rice in the middle of each shallow serving bowl and spoon 1 cup of gumbo over the top, making sure each person gets an assortment of the seafood and andouille. Serve half this amount in a cup as an appetizer.

Chicken and Smoked Sausage Gumbo

MAKES **6** MAIN-DISH OR **10** APPETIZER SERVINGS

There must be as many kinds of gumbo as there are families in south Louisiana! Maybe more, because each one has its own recipes using chicken, duck, sausage, beef, seafood, and vegetables, depending on what's available in their area. You know what? They're all great. And you know what else? I like my gumbo with a generous amount of creamy, rich, eggy potato salad right in the middle.

1 (2- to 3-pound) chicken, all
visible fat removed, cut into 8
pieces
2 tablespoons plus 2 teaspoons
Chef Paul Prudhomme's
Poultry Magic, *or 2 tablespoons*
Chef Paul Prudhomme's Meat
Magic, *in all*
1 cup finely diced onions
1 cup finely diced green bell peppers
¾ cup finely diced celery

1¼ cups all-purpose flour
Vegetable oil for deep-frying
7 cups chicken stock (see page 196)
½ pound andouille (preferred) or
top-quality smoked pork sausage,
diced into ¼-inch cubes
1 teaspoon minced fresh garlic
Salt and black pepper, optional
2 cups hot cooked white rice

Sprinkle the chicken evenly with *2 tablespoons* of the Poultry Magic (or 1 tablespoon plus 1 teaspoon of Meat Magic) and rub it in well. Let stand at room temperature while you dice the vegetables.

Combine the onions, bell peppers, and celery in a bowl and set aside.

Combine the remaining Poultry Magic (or Meat Magic) with the flour in a paper or plastic bag. Add the seasoned chicken pieces and shake until the chicken is well coated. Reserve ½ cup of the seasoned flour.

Heat 1½ inches of oil in a large, heavy skillet over high heat until very hot (375° to 400°), about 6 to 7 minutes. Fry the chicken, skin side down and large pieces first, until the crust is brown on both sides and the meat is cooked, about 5 to 8 minutes per side. You may have to fry the chicken in batches. Drain on paper towels. Carefully pour the hot oil into a heatproof glass measuring cup, leaving some of the brown bits in the pan, then return ½ cup of the hot oil to the pan.

Return the pan to high heat and gradually whisk in the reserved ½ cup seasoned flour. Cook, whisking constantly, until the roux is dark red-brown, about 3½ to 4 minutes, being careful not to let it scorch or splash on your skin. Remove the pan from the heat and immediately add the vegetables, stirring constantly until the roux stops getting darker. Place the pan over low heat and cook, stirring constantly and scraping the pan bottom well, until the vegetables are soft, about 5 minutes.

Meanwhile, bring the stock to a boil in a 5½-quart saucepan or Dutch oven. Add the vegetable mixture by spoonfuls to the boiling stock, stirring between each addition until the roux is dissolved. Return to a boil, stirring and scraping the pan bottom often. Reduce the heat to low, stir in the andouille and garlic, and simmer, uncovered, for 45 minutes, stirring often toward the end of the cooking time.

While the gumbo is simmering, pull the cooked chicken off the bones with your fingers and set it aside. When the gumbo has cooked for 45 minutes, stir in the chicken and adjust the seasoning, if desired, with salt and pepper. Serve immediately.

To serve as a main course, mound ⅓ cup cooked rice in the center of a shallow soup bowl and ladle about 1¼ cups gumbo around the rice. For an appetizer, place 1 heaping teaspoon cooked rice in a cup and ladle about ¾ cup gumbo on top.

Pot Luck

Red Flannel Hash

This dish, colored red by the beets, evolved years ago as a way to use up leftovers. With today's smaller families, we're not as likely to have a huge roast or corned beef that will serve a table full and still have 2½ cups of meat left over, but this hash is so good that we wouldn't want to wait for leftovers anyway. It's the best kind of one-dish meal, with meat, vegetable, and potato in one pan.

6 slices bacon, diced

1¾ cups chopped onions, in all

1 cup chopped celery

4 tablespoons unsalted butter

1 tablespoon plus 1 teaspoon **Chef Paul Prudhomme's Vegetable Magic,** in all

2 cups small diced peeled potatoes

1½ cups small diced fresh beets

2½ cups medium-diced cooked corned beef

½ cup loosely packed chopped fresh parsley

Cook the bacon over high heat in a 12-inch ovenproof skillet for 5 minutes. Add ¾ cup of the onions, stir, and cook until the onions start to brown, about 4 minutes. Add the celery, butter, 1 tablespoon of the Vegetable Magic, and the remaining 1 cup onions. Cook, stirring occasionally, for 6 minutes.

Preheat the broiler.

Stir in the potatoes, beets, corned beef, parsley, and the remaining 1 teaspoon Vegetable Magic and cook, stirring once or twice, until the mixture is sticking hard to the skillet but not burning, about 7 to 10 minutes.

Place the skillet under the broiler and broil until the hash is brown and bubbly, about 3 to 4 minutes.

Fried Green Tomatoes with Cream Gravy

MAKES 6 SERVINGS

Fried green tomatoes were an American classic long before the movie. They're popular in the Midwest and on the Atlantic Coast, but our favorite recipe comes from the South, where the tart green tomatoes are dredged in cornmeal. Don't slice the tomatoes too thin, or they won't hold together during the cooking process. These are great with eggs for breakfast or delicious for lunch, especially the way we serve them, on an English muffin.

¾ cup all-purpose flour
¼ cup yellow cornmeal
2 tablespoons **Chef Paul Prudhomme's Vegetable Magic**, in all
14 slices (about ¼ to ⅓ inch thick) very hard, very green (see Note) tomatoes (about 3 or 4 tomatoes)

8 slices bacon, diced
1 cup vegetable oil
1 cup chicken stock (see page 196)
1½ cups heavy cream, in all
6 English muffins, split

Combine the flour, cornmeal, and *1 tablespoon* of the Vegetable Magic in a small bowl.

Sprinkle the tomato slices evenly with a total of *2 teaspoons* Vegetable Magic and pat it in well.

Fry the bacon in a 12-inch skillet over high heat, stirring occasionally, for 3 minutes. Reduce the heat to medium and cook until the bacon is browned and crisp, about 4 to 5 minutes. Remove the bacon with a slotted spoon, drain, and set aside. Pour off the fat from the pan, reserving ¼ cup of the drippings.

Heat the reserved bacon drippings and the vegetable oil in the same skillet over high heat for 5 minutes. While the oil mixture is heating, dredge the seasoned tomato slices in the flour/cornmeal mixture, one at a time, and reserve the leftover flour mixture. When the oil mixture is hot, add 6 of the tomato slices, or as many as will fit in a single layer, and fry, turning twice, until browned, about 10 minutes. If the tomatoes brown too quickly, reduce the heat slightly. Remove with a slotted spatula and drain on paper towels. Fry the remaining tomato slices and drain them. Do not drain the oil mixture from the skillet. Chop 2 of the fried tomato slices and set aside.

Add 3 tablespoons of the reserved seasoned flour mixture to the oil in the skillet and cook, whisking constantly, for 3 minutes. Add the chopped tomatoes, stock, and cooked bacon and cook, whisking, for 2 minutes. Add *1 cup* of the cream and the remaining Vegetable Magic and cook, whisking, for 3 minutes. Whisk in the remaining ½ cup cream and remove from the heat.

To serve, toast the muffin halves. Place a tomato slice on each half and cover with ¼ cup of the gravy.

NOTE: It may be difficult to find really hard green tomatoes. Ask the produce manager where you shop if they are available in your area. They may have to be special ordered.

Eye-Opener Omelet

MAKES **2** SERVINGS

☆☆☆☆☆☆☆

This delicious omelet is worth getting up for any day! It's also great as a light lunch or supper, and when serving it, I like to offer a little extra Magic Pepper Sauce to really open an eye.

1 tablespoon plus 2 teaspoons margarine or unsalted butter, in all

¼ cup chopped onions

¼ cup chopped celery

¼ cup chopped green bell peppers

1 tablespoon plus 2 teaspoons **Chef Paul Prudhomme's Poultry Magic,** in all

2 teaspoons minced fresh garlic

½ cup canned crushed tomatoes

½ cup chicken stock (see page 196)

6 large eggs, in all

¼ cup milk, in all

½ teaspoon **Chef Paul Prudhomme's Magic Pepper Sauce,** in all

Melt 1 tablespoon of the margarine or butter in a heavy 10-inch skillet over high heat. When it sizzles, add the onions, celery, bell peppers, and *1 tablespoon* of the Poultry Magic. Cook and stir for 2 minutes, then stir in the garlic. Reduce the heat to medium and cook, stirring and scraping as the vegetables brown and start to stick, for 2 minutes more. Stir in the tomatoes and cook for 1½ minutes. Add the stock and cook, stirring occasionally, until the vegetables are soft and the sauce is thick, about 15 minutes. Remove from the heat.

This recipe makes enough sauce for 2 omelets, but each omelet is made individually. For the first omelet, whip together *3 eggs, 2 tablespoons* milk, *1 teaspoon* Poultry Magic, and *¼ teaspoon* Magic Pepper Sauce until frothy.

Melt *1 teaspoon* margarine or butter in a heavy 9-inch skillet over medium-high heat. When it sizzles, add the egg mixture and cook until the eggs begin to set, about 30 seconds. As soon as there is a base of cooked egg on the bottom, use a spatula to pull the eggs from the outer edge of the pan toward the middle, giving the uncooked egg mixture a chance to cook. Continue pulling the cooked portion toward the center of the pan, cooking for about 2 minutes, or until the eggs are almost cooked through. The top should still be a little loose. Spoon about ¼ cup of the sauce over half the omelet and fold the other side over to form a half-moon shape. Carefully slide the omelet onto a serving plate, and spoon another ¼ cup sauce on top. Repeat with the remaining ingredients to make the other omelet. Serve immediately.

SEE COLOR PHOTOGRAPH

Sweet Potato Omelet

☆☆☆☆☆☆

My hometown, Opelousas, Louisiana, is the sweet potato capital of the world. Every year at the end of harvest, we devote a week to a festival we call the Yambilee. It's a week filled with cooking contests, parades, beauty contests, battles of the bands, and lots of fun activities. One of my vivid memories of the Yambilee is the literally hundreds of ways that sweet potatoes can be cooked. We fried, baked, boiled, creamed, mashed, and even stepped on them. There was even a dance called Lache-pas la Patate ("Don't Drop the Potato") during which couples held a sweet potato between their foreheads while they danced. The object was not to lose control of the potato, and the couples got into some very humorous positions to keep the potato from falling.

This recipe is one of my all-time favorite sweet-potato-eating experiences.

2 (6- to 8-ounce) sweet potatoes, baked until just fork tender (keep firm)

1 tablespoon dark brown sugar

1 (5- to 7-ounce) white potato, baked until just fork tender (keep firm)

6 eggs

½ cup evaporated milk or heavy cream

⅓ cup chicken fat or vegetable oil

¾ cup diced tasso (preferred) or other smoked ham (such as Cure 81)

½ cup julienne onions (see page 4)

½ cup julienne green bell peppers (see page 4)

1 tablespoon **Chef Paul Prudhomme's Meat Magic**

½ cup julienne yellow squash (see page 4)

½ cup julienne zucchini (see page 4)

Peel the baked sweet potatoes, dice into ½-inch cubes, and place in a small bowl with the brown sugar. Stir to combine well. Peel the baked white potato, dice into ½-inch cubes, and set aside.

Whisk the eggs in a medium-size bowl until frothy, then blend in the milk or cream.

Preheat the broiler.

In a 10-inch ovenproof skillet with 2-inch sides, heat the fat or oil over high heat until hot, 1 to 2 minutes. Add the tasso and white potatoes and cook, stirring occasionally, for 1 minute. Add the onions, bell peppers, and Meat Magic, and cook, stirring occasionally and scraping the pan bottom well, for 3 minutes. Stir in the squash and zucchini and continue cooking, stirring occasionally and scraping the pan bottom well, for 3 minutes. Stir in the sweet potatoes and cook and stir for 2 minutes more.

Whisk the egg mixture briefly again and add it to the skillet. Cook for 30 seconds while pushing the mixture toward the center of the pan with a spatula. Distribute all ingredients evenly in the pan, remove from the heat, and place under the broiler, 4 to 5 inches from the heat source. Cook until the eggs are almost set and beginning to brown around the edges, about 2 minutes. The time will vary depending upon how close the omelet is to the heat source. Remove from the broiler and let the pan sit for a minute or two, so that the eggs will finish cooking by residual heat, and serve immediately.

Egg Foo Yung

MAKES **8** SERVINGS

★ ★ ★ ★ ★ ☆

The combination of tastes and textures of the fresh seafood and crunchy sprouts makes this Chinese-American dish practically irresistible. It's very important to stir the ingredients every time just before ladling the mixture into the skillet, to be sure there's enough of the egg to hold everything else together during cooking. Don't worry, however, if your egg foo yung falls apart—it will be just as delicious.

6 to 12 tablespoons peanut oil,
  in all

1 cup diced ham, about 4 ounces

1 tablespoon plus 1 teaspoon
  minced fresh ginger

1 cup chopped green onion tops

1½ teaspoons minced fresh garlic

4 cups fresh sunflower, mung, or
  soybean sprouts (see Note)

1 pound lump crabmeat, picked
  over for shell and cartilage

1 pound peeled small shrimp

2 tablespoons plus 1 teaspoon **Chef
  Paul Prudhomme's Seafood
  Magic**

½ teaspoon ground ginger

8 eggs

Place *3 tablespoons* of the oil and the ham in a 10-inch skillet over high heat and cook, stirring occasionally, until the ham is lightly browned, about 4 minutes. Add the fresh ginger, green onion tops, and garlic and cook until the vegetables are lightly browned, about 4 to 5 minutes. Turn off the heat, transfer the contents of the skillet to a large bowl, and add the sprouts, crabmeat, shrimp, Seafood Magic, and ground ginger.

Beat the eggs until frothy in a separate bowl and gently fold them into the cooked vegetables until well blended.

Heat *3 tablespoons* of the oil in an 8- or 10-inch skillet over high heat. Stir the egg mixture and ladle about ½ cup per omelet into the skillet; cook the omelets, 2 at a time, until golden brown on both sides. Stir the mixture just before ladling each omelet and add oil to the skillet as needed, letting it get hot before cooking the next omelets.

Drain the omelets on paper towels and serve immediately with or without soy sauce.

NOTE: If you can't find these sprouts, you can use whatever are available at your market, such as radish or alfalfa sprouts. The ones we mention, however, are larger and juicier and give the omelets an exciting texture.

★

Chicken and Tasso Jambalaya

MAKES **4** MAIN-DISH OR **8** APPETIZER SERVINGS

As with gumbo, there are many varieties of jambalaya in south Louisiana, depending upon what is readily available in each area—and what a particular family likes best. In fact, you'll probably not find any two people who make it exactly the same way, but just about all versions are wonderful. This jambalaya is one of the most traditional kinds.

continued

SEASONING MIX
2 tablespoons **Chef Paul
Prudhomme's Poultry Magic,** or
**Chef Paul Prudhomme's Meat
Magic,** or **Chef Paul
Prudhomme's Pork and Veal
Magic**
2 bay leaves
¼ teaspoon rubbed sage

•

2 tablespoons unsalted butter
½ pound chopped tasso (preferred)
or other smoked ham, about 2
cups (see page 3)

¾ pound boneless chicken, cut into
bite-size pieces, about 2 cups
1 cup chopped onions, in all
1 cup chopped celery, in all
1 cup chopped green bell peppers,
in all
1 tablespoon minced fresh garlic
½ cup tomato sauce
1 cup peeled (see page 3) and
chopped fresh tomatoes
2½ cups chicken stock
(see page 196)
1½ cups uncooked rice (preferably
converted)

Combine the seasoning mix ingredients in a small bowl.

Melt the butter in a 2-quart saucepan over high heat. Add the tasso and cook, stirring frequently, until the meat starts to brown, about 3 minutes. Add the chicken and continue cooking, stirring frequently and scraping the pan bottom well, until the chicken is browned, about 3 to 5 minutes. Stir in the seasoning mix, ½ *cup each* of the onions, celery, and bell peppers, and the garlic.

Preheat the oven to 350°.

Continue to cook the mixture, stirring almost constantly and scraping the pan bottom as needed, until the vegetables start to get tender, about 5 to 8 minutes. Stir in the tomato sauce and cook, stirring often, for 1 minute. Stir in the remaining onions, celery, and bell peppers and the tomatoes. Remove from the heat, stir in the stock and rice, and mix well. Transfer the mixture to an ungreased 8×8-inch baking pan and bake, uncovered, until the rice is tender but still a bit crunchy, about 40 minutes. Remove from the oven, stir well, and discard the bay leaves. Let sit for 5 minutes before serving.

Chicken and Seafood Jambalaya

MAKES 4 MAIN-DISH OR 8 APPETIZER SERVINGS

I never tire of jambalaya. It's a great rice dish with a smoky flavor and an explosion of taste. One of the stories that the staff at K-Paul's likes to tell is about me putting a great heap of jambalaya on coconut cake as a snack.

2½ tablespoons chicken or beef fat, pork lard, butter, or oil

⅔ cup chopped tasso (preferred) or other smoked ham, about 3 ounces (see page 3)

½ cup chopped andouille (preferred) or any other good pure pork smoked sausage, about 3 ounces (see page 3)

1½ cups chopped onions

1 cup chopped celery

¾ cup chopped green bell peppers

½ cup bite-size pieces chicken, about 3 ounces

2 tablespoons **Chef Paul Prudhomme's Seafood Magic** or **Chef Paul Prudhomme's Poultry Magic** or **Chef Paul Prudhomme's Meat Magic**

2 bay leaves

1½ teaspoons minced fresh garlic

4 medium-size fresh tomatoes, peeled (see page 3) and chopped, about 1 pound

¾ cup tomato sauce

2 cups seafood stock (see page 194)

½ cup chopped green onions

2 cups uncooked rice (preferably converted)

1½ dozen peeled medium shrimp, about ½ pound

1½ dozen shucked medium oysters in their liquor (the liquid in which they're packed), about 10 ounces

continued

Melt the fat in a 4-quart saucepan over medium heat. Add the tasso and andouille and cook, stirring frequently, until crisp, about 5 to 8 minutes. Add the onions, celery, and bell peppers and cook, stirring occasionally and scraping the pan bottom well, until tender but still firm, about 5 minutes. Add the chicken, raise the heat to high, and cook, stirring constantly, for 1 minute. Reduce the heat to medium and add the Magic Seasoning Blends, bay leaves, and garlic. Cook, stirring constantly and scraping the pan bottom as needed, for 3 minutes. Add the tomatoes and cook, stirring frequently, until the chicken is tender, about 5 to 8 minutes.

Preheat the oven to 350°.

Add the tomato sauce to the saucepan and continue to cook, stirring fairly often, for 7 minutes. Stir in the stock, bring to a boil, then stir in the green onions. Cook, stirring once or twice, for 2 minutes. Add the rice, shrimp, and oysters, stir well, and remove from the heat. Transfer to an ungreased 8×8-inch baking pan, cover snugly with aluminum foil, and bake until the rice is tender but still a bit crunchy, about 20 minutes. Remove from the oven and let stand, covered, for 10 minutes. Discard the bay leaves and serve immediately.

Shepherd's Pie

As you might guess from its name, this dish had its origins in sheep-raising regions of the world. We've adapted it from the humble lamb casserole it used to be and spiced it up with Magic Pepper Sauce and Meat Magic. It reheats well, which makes it perfect for covered-dish suppers.

1½ pounds ground beef

½ pound ground pork

2 eggs, lightly beaten

½ cup very fine dry bread crumbs

¼ pound (1 stick) plus 3 tablespoons unsalted butter, in all

¾ cup finely diced onions

¾ cup finely diced celery

½ cup finely diced green bell peppers

1 tablespoon plus 1 teaspoon minced garlic

1 tablespoon Worcestershire sauce

½ teaspoon **Chef Paul Prudhomme's Magic Pepper Sauce**

2 tablespoons Chef Paul Prudhomme's Meat Magic

¾ cup evaporated milk, in all

2 pounds white potatoes, peeled and quartered

1 teaspoon salt

1 teaspoon white pepper

1½ cups julienne carrots (see page 4)

1 cup julienne onions (see page 4)

1 teaspoon Chef Paul Prudhomme's Vegetable Magic

1½ cups julienne zucchini (see page 4)

1 cup julienne yellow squash (see page 4)

continued

Combine the beef and pork in an ungreased 13×9-inch baking pan. Mix in the eggs and bread crumbs by hand until thoroughly combined and set aside.

Preheat the oven to 450°.

In a 1-quart saucepan, combine *3 tablespoons* of the butter, the onions, celery, bell peppers, garlic, Worcestershire sauce, Magic Pepper Sauce, and Meat Magic. Cook over high heat, stirring frequently and scraping the pan bottom well, for 5 minutes. Remove from the heat, let cool, and add to the meat mixture, along with *¼ cup* of the milk. Mix well by hand and form into a 12×8-inch loaf and center in the pan (the meat loaf will not quite touch the sides of the pan). Bake until browned on top, about 30 minutes, then remove from the oven. Pour off the drippings, reserving 2 tablespoons plus 1½ teaspoons. Set the meat and reserved drippings aside.

Meanwhile, boil the potatoes until fork tender. Drain, reserving 1 cup of the cooking water. Place the hot potatoes in a large mixing bowl with the remaining 1 stick butter, ½ cup milk, and the salt and pepper. Stir with a wooden spoon until broken up, then beat with a whisk (or electric mixer with a paddle) until creamy and velvety smooth. If the potatoes are not creamy enough, mix in a little of the reserved cooking water.

In a large skillet, preferably nonstick, combine the reserved drippings with the carrots, onions, and Vegetable Magic and sauté over high heat, stirring frequently, for 1½ minutes. Add the zucchini and yellow squash and continue cooking until the vegetables are noticeably brighter in color, about 3 to 4 minutes. Remove from the heat.

Raise the oven temperature to 525°.

Mound the undrained vegetables on top of the meat loaf, away from the edges. Layer all the mashed potatoes evenly over the top of the vegetables and top edges of the meat. Bake until browned on top, about 8 to 10 minutes, and serve immediately.

Nice Rice, Keen Beans, and Pastabilities

Spanish Rice

This colorful, flavorful dish goes well with almost any meat, fish, or poultry, but I think it's especially delicious with grilled andouille, a hot smoked sausage from Louisiana. Balance with a nice green salad and you've got a meal that's easy to prepare, looks great, and tastes terrific.

10 slices bacon, diced

4 tablespoons **Chef Paul Prudhomme's Pork and Veal Magic**

2 bay leaves

2 cups chopped onions

1½ cups chopped green bell peppers

1 cup chopped celery

2½ cups uncooked quick-cooking rice

1 (16-ounce) can tomatoes, chopped

1 teaspoon minced fresh garlic

5 cups chicken stock (see page 196)

¼ cup finely minced fresh parsley

Cook the bacon in a heavy 5-quart pot over high heat until it starts to brown, about 5 to 6 minutes. Add the Pork and Veal Magic, bay leaves, onions, peppers, and celery. Cover and cook until the onions are golden brown, about 12 to 14 minutes.

Stir in the rice, cover, and cook, occasionally scraping up the crust that forms on the bottom of the pot, until the rice is golden brown, about 5 minutes. Stir in the tomatoes, mashing them with a spoon, then mix in the garlic; cover and cook for 2 minutes. Add the stock and scrape the bottom of the pot.

Cover, bring to a boil, reduce the heat to low, and simmer for about 10 to 12 minutes. Stir in the parsley, remove from the heat, and let sit, covered, for 10 minutes before serving.

San Francisco Rice

An interesting side note about this dish is that its distinctive ingredients—rice and spaghetti—are the gifts of two immigrant cultures of old San Francisco, the Chinese and the Italians. Browning the rice and spaghetti, along with the vegetables, in the hot oil gives a true taste of what happens with high-temperature cooking in a wok.

SEASONING MIX
2 tablespoons plus ½ teaspoon
   Chef Paul Prudhomme's
   Vegetable Magic
1½ teaspoons dried cilantro leaves
¾ teaspoon ground ginger

•

¼ cup peanut oil
1 cup uncooked converted long-
   grain rice

1 cup 2-inch pieces uncooked #4
   spaghetti
2 cups chopped onions
1 cup chopped celery
2 tablespoons unsalted butter
¼ cup sesame seeds
2 teaspoons minced fresh garlic
½ cup chopped fresh parsley
3 cups chicken stock (see page 196)

Combine the seasoning mix ingredients in a small bowl.

Heat the oil in a 12-inch skillet over high heat until very hot, about 4 minutes. Add the rice, spaghetti, onions, celery, butter, and *1 tablespoon plus 1 teaspoon* of the seasoning mix. Stir well and cook, shaking the pan and stirring occasionally, until the rice and spaghetti are golden brown, about 6 minutes. Add the sesame seeds and the remaining seasoning mix. Stir well and cook for 2 minutes. Add the garlic and cook, stirring occasionally, until the rice and spaghetti are browned, about 3 to 5 minutes. Stir in the parsley and stock, cover the skillet, and bring to a boil over high heat. Reduce the heat to low and simmer for 12 minutes. Remove from the heat and let sit, covered, for 8 minutes before serving.

☆

Fresh Garlic Pasta

MAKES **4** SERVINGS

Quick and easy to make, this delicious dish goes wonderfully with roast meat and a fresh vegetable salad.

3 tablespoons olive oil

6 cloves fresh garlic, sliced lengthwise into thirds

2 tablespoons unsalted butter

*1 tablespoon plus 1 teaspoon **Chef Paul Prudhomme's Poultry Magic***

½ cup chopped green onions

5 cups cooked pasta (your favorite)

In a 12-inch skillet, heat the oil to 200° and add the garlic. Cook until the garlic starts to brown at the edges. Add the butter and Pork and Veal Magic and cook until the garlic turns golden brown. Add the onions and pasta, toss, and cook until the pasta is thoroughly heated. Serve immediately.

Lentils and Rice

MAKES 8 CUPS, ENOUGH FOR 8 SIDE-DISH OR 4 MAIN-DISH SERVINGS

The rich, earthy taste of lentils goes perfectly with all the wonderful varieties of rice on the market today.

2½ cups chopped onions, in all
1 cup chopped green bell peppers
8 ounces finely diced turkey tasso
  or your favorite smoked ham
  (see page 3)
1½ cups dried lentils
1 tablespoon **Chef Paul
  Prudhomme's Seafood Magic**

1 tablespoon **Chef Paul
  Prudhomme's Meat Magic**
½ cup chopped celery
1½ cups short-grain white rice
  (see Note)
7 cups chicken stock (see page 196)

Preheat a heavy 5-quart pot, preferably nonstick, over high heat for 4 minutes. Add *1½ cups* of the onions and all the bell peppers and cook, scraping the bottom of the pot once or twice, until the vegetables start to brown, about 5 minutes. Stir in the tasso, lentils, and the Magic Seasonings and cook for 2 minutes. Add the celery and the remaining onions, mix, and cook for 2 more minutes. Stir in the rice and cook for 2 to 3 minutes. Add the stock and scrape the bottom and sides of the pot. Bring to a boil, reduce the heat to low, cover, and cook until the rice is done and the lentils are tender, about 35 to 40 minutes.

NOTE: If you are not using converted rice, first wash it in a bowl of cool water, rubbing it between your hands for 2 or 3 minutes, then drain thoroughly.

SEE COLOR PHOTOGRAPH

Pasta Primavera

MAKES **6** TO **8** SERVINGS

★☆★☆★☆

Primavera means "spring," and this pasta dish takes its name from the tender young asparagus tips or snow peas that once were available only in early spring. Now, thanks to modern all-weather farming methods and the rapid transportation of produce, you can enjoy this treat any time of year. Leave out the prosciutto for a great vegetarian dish.

9 ounces uncooked pasta (your favorite)

2 tablespoons olive oil

1 cup thin strips prosciutto, about ¼ pound

2 cups cauliflower florets

2 cups sliced fresh mushrooms

½ cup diagonally sliced carrots

2 cups sliced zucchini

6 tablespoons unsalted butter

1 teaspoon minced fresh garlic

*3 tablespoons plus 1 teaspoon **Chef Paul Prudhomme's Pork and Veal Magic***

1 cup asparagus tips, or ¾ cup snow peas

1 cup chopped green onions

3 cups heavy cream

Cook the pasta according to package directions, drain, and set aside.

Heat the oil in a 12-inch skillet over high heat. When the oil is very hot, add the prosciutto, cauliflower, mushrooms, carrots, and zucchini. Add the butter, and as it melts, stir in the garlic and Pork and Veal Magic. Stir in the asparagus tips or snow peas and the green onions, mix well, and cook just until the vegetables are crisp-tender, about 4 to 5 minutes. Stir in the cream and bring to a boil. Lower the heat to medium and cook until the sauce thickens a bit, about 3 minutes.

Add the drained pasta, toss well, and serve immediately.

Rice and Cheese Casserole

MAKES 10 SERVINGS

★ ☆ ☆ ☆ ☆ ☆

This dish is perfect for those times when you're hungry for something cheesy and filling, yet want to eat something low in fat. You can enjoy all you want of this casserole with a clear conscience! Unless you grow your own greens and can pick just the quantities you need, you will have some left over. But that's great, because you can cook the spinach or collards for another meal or use the spinach and lettuce for a healthful and delicious salad.

SEASONING MIX

3 tablespoons **Chef Paul Prudhomme's Poultry Magic**

2 teaspoons dry mustard

¼ teaspoon ground nutmeg

•

1 pound coarsely ground turkey

2 cups chopped onions

2 cups chopped green bell peppers

1 cup chopped celery

5 cups defatted chicken stock, in all (see page 2)

2 cups chopped green leaf lettuce

2 cups chopped red leaf lettuce

2 cups chopped fresh spinach

1 cup chopped collard greens

2½ cups uncooked long-grain white rice

•

CHEESE MIXTURE

4 ounces low-fat cream cheese

2 ounces low-fat mozzarella cheese

1 cup low-fat sour cream

2 ounces Cheddar-flavored soya cheese substitute

1 tablespoon lemon juice

•

6 ounces reduced-fat Jarlsberg or other semisoft white cheese, sliced

Combine the seasoning mix ingredients in a small bowl.

Sprinkle *1 tablespoon plus 1 teaspoon* of the seasoning mix evenly over the ground turkey and mix well.

Preheat a heavy 5-quart pot, preferably nonstick, over high heat for 4 minutes. Add the onions, bell peppers, celery, and *2 tablespoons* of the seasoning mix. Cook, scraping the bottom of the pot frequently, for 6 minutes. Add *½ cup* of the stock, scrape the bottom of the pot clean, and cook until the liquid evaporates and the vegetables stick to the bottom, about 7 minutes. Add another *½ cup* stock, scrape the bottom of the pot clean, and move the vegetables to the outside edges of the pot. Add the seasoned turkey to the center of the pot and cook, stirring frequently, until it browns, about 15 minutes. Add the remaining stock, the chopped greens, and the remaining seasoning mix, bring to a boil, and add the rice. Return to a boil, reduce the heat to low, and simmer, covered, for 17 minutes.

Meanwhile, place all the ingredients for the cheese mixture into a blender and process until completely blended and smooth.

Preheat the oven to 350°.

When the rice is done, place ⅓ of the rice mixture in a 5-quart casserole, cover evenly with half of the cheese mixture, and repeat the process, ending with the last ⅓ of the rice mixture. Cover evenly with the sliced Jarlsberg cheese and bake, covered, for 20 minutes.

Dirty Rice

This recipe was named not for real dirt but for all the little bits of ground meat that give it its color. If I had to list the dishes in my very favorite meal, this wonderful Louisiana specialty would definitely be included, along with roast pork, candied yams, and potato salad.

2 tablespoons chicken fat (preferred)
  or vegetable oil
½ pound ground chicken gizzards
¼ pound ground pork
2 bay leaves
2 tablespoons plus 1 teaspoon **Chef Paul Prudhomme's Poultry Magic**
1 teaspoon dry mustard
1 teaspoon ground cumin
½ cup finely diced onions

½ cup finely diced celery
½ cup finely diced green bell
  peppers
2 teaspoons minced fresh garlic
2 tablespoons unsalted butter
¾ cup uncooked rice (preferably
  converted)
2 cups chicken or pork stock
  (see page 196 or 198)
⅓ pound ground chicken livers

Place the chicken fat (or oil), gizzards, pork, and bay leaves in a large, heavy skillet, preferably nonstick, over high heat and stir well. Cook, stirring occasionally, until the meat is thoroughly browned, about 7 to 10 minutes. Stir in the Poultry Magic, mustard, and cumin, then add the onions, celery, bell peppers, and garlic. Stir thoroughly, scraping the pan bottom well, then add the butter and stir until melted. Reduce the heat to medium and cook, stirring constantly and scraping the pan bottom well, for 4 minutes. Add the rice and cook, constantly stirring and scraping the pan bottom, for 4 minutes, or until the rice starts to crackle and pop.

Add the stock and stir to loosen any bits stuck to the bottom of the pan, then cook over high heat, stirring occasionally, for 4 minutes. Stir in the chicken livers, cover the pan, and reduce the heat to very low. Cook for 10 minutes, remove from the heat, and leave covered until the rice is tender, about 10 minutes. (The rice is finished this way to preserve the delicate flavor of the livers by not overcooking them.) Remove the bay leaves and serve immediately.

SEE COLOR PHOTOGRAPH

Monday Red Beans

MAKES ABOUT 7 CUPS, ENOUGH FOR 4 GENEROUS SERVINGS OVER RICE

Red beans with rice is the traditional Monday supper in New Orleans. Monday was always wash day, and the beans could simmer all day on the back burner of the stove without a whole lot of attention. When the laundry was done, so were the beans. Nowadays it's the custom for almost everyone, including people who never do their own laundry, to enjoy red beans and rice every Monday. This recipe keeps well and is just as good a couple of days later.

continued

½ pound dried red kidney beans

About 10 cups water, in all

3 pounds small ham hocks

1¼ cups finely chopped celery

1 cup finely chopped onions

1 cup finely chopped green bell
  peppers

3 bay leaves

1½ teaspoons **Chef Paul
  Prudhomme's Magic Pepper
  Sauce**

1 tablespoon plus 2 teaspoons **Chef
  Paul Prudhomme's Meat Magic**

Add enough water to the beans to cover them by 3 or 4 inches and soak overnight in the refrigerator.

Place *8 cups* of water, the ham hocks, celery, onions, bell peppers, and bay leaves in a 5½-quart saucepan or Dutch oven. Stir well, cover, and bring to a boil over high heat. Remove the cover, reduce the heat, and simmer for 1 hour, stirring occasionally. Raise the heat and boil, stirring occasionally, until the meat falls off the bones, about 15 to 20 minutes. Remove the meat and bones; set the meat aside and discard the bones.

Drain the beans and add them and the remaining 2 cups of water to the pot, along with the Magic Pepper Sauce and the Meat Magic. Bring to a boil, reduce the heat, and simmer, stirring occasionally and scraping the bottom of the pot fairly often, until the beans are tender and start breaking up, about 1 hour. Return the meat to the pot, stir, and cook 10 minutes more. Discard the bay leaves and break up any large pieces of meat. Serve over cooked long-grain white rice, with Magic Pepper Sauce on the side for those who like a little more heat.

SEE COLOR PHOTOGRAPH

Chickpeas, Chicken, and Mushrooms

MAKES **4** SERVINGS

There's absolutely nothing difficult about this recipe, but please notice that the chickpeas are soaked overnight. Chickpeas, or garbanzos as they are also called, are used in cooking in many parts of the world. They're very nourishing and are a good source of protein.

1½ cups dried chickpeas

SEASONING MIX
*2 tablespoons **Chef Paul***
  Prudhomme's Poultry Magic
2 teaspoons dried sweet basil leaves
½ teaspoon ground nutmeg

2 pounds chicken breast, diced
3 cups chopped onions, in all
5 cups sliced fresh mushrooms,
  in all
3½ cups defatted chicken stock, in
  all (see page 2)
1 tablespoon minced fresh garlic

•

DAY 1 • Add enough water to the chickpeas to cover them by 3 or 4 inches, and soak overnight in the refrigerator. As the peas absorb the water, they will more than double in volume.

DAY 2 • Combine the seasoning mix ingredients in a small bowl.
  Preheat a heavy 5-quart pot, preferably nonstick, over high heat to 350°, about 4 minutes.

continued

Drain but do not rinse the chickpeas.

Sprinkle the chicken evenly with *2 tablespoons* of the seasoning mix and rub it in well. Place the chicken in the pot and cook, stirring as necessary, until it is browned on all sides, about 6 minutes. Remove the chicken and set it aside. Reduce the heat to medium, add *1 cup* of the onions and all the chickpeas to the pot, stir, and cook for 5 minutes.

Return the heat to high and add *2 cups* of the mushrooms and *½ cup* stock. Scrape the pan bottom and cook for 10 to 12 minutes. Add the remaining seasoning mix, onions, stock, and mushrooms, along with the garlic and chicken, and cook until the chicken is completely done, about 15 minutes.

Blackening and Bronzing

☆☆☆☆☆☆

When I developed the blackening method of cooking—using redfish at the beginning but later other kinds of fish, fowl, and meat—I truly had no idea how popular (and imitated) it would become! Over the years I have perfected this technique, and the following are my most up-to-date and current recipes and cooking tips. It's really a simple technique, and one that produces exciting results.

Remember that these recipes should only be used with the very freshest products available. This cooking method attaches flavors to the outside of the food being cooked. The fresh flavor of the product will result in a beautifully flavored dish—a poor or old product will create a poorly flavored dish.

BLACKENING

For blackening, you need a cast-iron skillet to stand up to the intense heat. And because the method produces a great deal of heat and smoke, unless you have a commercial kitchen range hood, you'll want to work outdoors on a gas grill or burner.

Here's the procedure for blackening:

- Melt unsalted butter or margarine in a pan or skillet large enough to hold whatever you're going to cook, then set it aside to cool. Heat a large cast-iron skillet over very high heat until it is extremely hot, at least 500°. It will take about 10 minutes to heat.

- The item to be blackened should be at room temperature (so the butter will adhere but not congeal). If you must use cold meat or fish, you will have to adjust the cooking time and turn the item almost continuously to avoid burning and to lock in the juices. Turning the item continuously forces the juices to remain in the center. For example, when you see the little drops of juice appear on the top of a grilling hamburger, they are being pushed up by the heat underneath.

- Dip the item in the melted butter so that both sides are lightly and evenly coated. Sprinkle (don't pour) the desired Magic Seasoning Blend

Blackening and Bronzing Table

MAGIC SEASONING BLEND	TYPES OF MEAT, FISH, OR POULTRY
Blackened Redfish Magic, Seafood Magic, or Meat Magic	Redfish, pompano, red snapper fillets, salmon steaks, or any firm-fleshed fish, about ½ to ¾ inch thick
Blackened Steak Magic or Meat Magic	Prime rib, sirloin steak, ribeye, porterhouse, filet mignon, about 1 inch thick; hamburgers (ground meat, chuck, sirloin), about ¾ to 1 inch thick
Pork and Veal Magic or Meat Magic	Pork chops, veal chops, lamb chops, about ¾ to 1 inch thick
Poultry Magic or Meat Magic	Chicken or turkey, boned and pounded flat to ½ inch thick

on one side of the fish (or bird or meat) and carefully place it, seasoned side down, in the hot, dry skillet. Sprinkle the top with Magic Seasoning Blend.

• Cook, turning frequently, until done. The cooking time will vary according to what you are blackening, but 4 minutes total cooking time is usual.

That's it! Because the method is simple, any variation will make a dramatic difference. Be sure the skillet is hot enough and absolutely dry. Be sure not to overseason—the herbs and spices should highlight the taste rather than hide it. And you don't want to overcook the fillet, chop, or steak—there's a big difference between blackened and burned. Avoid a burned, bitter taste by wiping out the skillet between batches.

BRONZING

The method for bronzing is the same as for blackening except that the pan should be heated only to 350°, which takes about 4 minutes. Bronzing can be done indoors. Because the temperature is lower, you'll cook each piece of fish (or bird or meat) a little longer. Watch the first fillet you cook to determine the best time for the variety you're bronzing.

The key to bronzing is to keep the skillet as close to 350° as possible, a simple matter if you use an electric skillet or a skillet thermometer, available at kitchen gadget shops. You can still judge the approximate temperature even if you're bronzing with a rangetop skillet. If the temperature drops too low, which will produce less taste and more dryness, you'll notice that the food cooks very slowly. When bronzing is done properly at 350°, it cooks about as fast as it would if there were oil in the skillet. If the temperature rises too far above 350°, blue smoke will rise, which indicates that the temperature is too high for bronzing.

So remember: Do not overcook! Do not overseason!

If you want a low-fat dish, you'll be glad to know that both blackening and bronzing can be done without butter or oil. Simply omit the butter and use the same skillets you would if you were using butter—cast-iron for blackening and nonstick for bronzing.

Blackened Chicken Breasts

Most of us eat a lot of chicken. It's not expensive and we know it's low in fat, especially the breast. One of my assistants says she cooks so much chicken for her children that whenever she tries a new way her son announces, "Chicken Number 467" or whatever. Now here's a way of cooking chicken that changes the taste into something totally different. Just remember that blackening produces so much heat and smoke that it must be done outdoors or in a commercial restaurant kitchen.

2 ounces (½ stick) unsalted butter
6 (4- to 5-ounce) chicken breasts, boned and pounded flat to ½ inch thick, at room temperature (see Note)

*1 tablespoon **Chef Paul Prudhomme's Poultry Magic** or **Chef Paul Prudhomme's Meat Magic***

Melt the butter in a pan or skillet large enough to hold one breast and set it aside, allowing it to cool slightly.

Heat a large cast-iron skillet over very high heat until it is extremely hot—at least 500°, which will take about 10 minutes.

Be sure the chicken is at room temperature (so the butter will adhere but not congeal). Dip the breasts in the melted butter so that both sides are lightly and evenly coated. Place the chicken on a plate and sprinkle (don't pour) ¼ teaspoon Poultry (or Meat) Magic on one side of each breast. Carefully place the breasts, seasoned side down, in the hot, dry skillet. Sprinkle the remaining seasoning on the top of the breasts and cook, turning frequently, until done. Be careful not to cook too long. Overcooking will cause the chicken to become dry. Serve piping hot.

If you find it necessary to cook the chicken in batches because of the size of your skillet, clean the skillet after each batch by quickly wiping it out with a clean, dry cloth. Bring it back to the extreme high heat before cooking the remaining breasts. Wiping out the skillet between batches will help eliminate a burned taste.

That's it! Because the method is simple, any variation will make a dramatic difference. Be sure the skillet is hot enough and absolutely dry. Be sure not to overseason—the seasoning should highlight the taste rather than hide it. And you don't want to overcook the breasts—there's a big difference between blackened and burned.

NOTE: If you must use cold meat, you will have to adjust the cooking time and turn the breasts almost continuously to avoid burning.

If you want a low-fat dish, you'll be glad to know that blackening can be done without butter or oil. Simply omit the butter and use the same skillet you would if you were using butter.

Blackened Steak

☆ ☆ ☆ ☆ ☆ ☆

You can't imagine how exciting beef can taste until you bite into a blackened steak! Don't misunderstand—I have nothing against charcoal broiling, but the crust that blackening gives a steak just can't be duplicated with any other cooking method, and I think it adds a whole new dimension to the taste of the meat. Blackening, like charcoal broiling, must be done outside or in a commercial restaurant kitchen.

Up to ¼ pound (1 stick) unsalted
   butter
6 steaks (prime rib, sirloin, ribeye,
   porterhouse, or filet mignon), each
   about 1 inch thick, at room
   temperature (see Note)

1 tablespoon **Chef Paul
Prudhomme's Blackened Steak
Magic** or **Chef Paul
Prudhomme's Meat Magic**

Melt the butter in a pan or skillet large enough to hold one steak and set it aside to cool slightly.

Heat a large cast-iron skillet over very high heat until it is extremely hot, at least 500°. It will take about 10 minutes to heat.

Be sure the meat is at room temperature (so the butter will adhere but not congeal). Dip the steaks in the melted butter so that both sides are lightly and evenly coated. Place the meat on a plate and sprinkle (don't pour) ¼ teaspoon Blackened Steak (or Meat) Magic on one side of each steak. Carefully place the steaks in the hot, dry skillet with the seasoned side down. Sprinkle with the remaining seasoning and cook, turning frequently, until they cook to the desired doneness. Be careful not to cook too long. Serve piping hot.

If you find it necessary to cook the steaks in batches because of the size of your skillet, clean the skillet after each batch by quickly wiping it out with a clean, dry cloth. Bring it back to the extreme high heat before cooking the remaining steaks. Wiping out the skillet between batches will help eliminate a burned taste.

That's it! Because the method is simple, any variation will make a dramatic difference. Be sure the skillet is hot enough and absolutely dry. Be sure not to overseason—the seasoning should highlight the taste rather than hide it. And you don't want to overcook the steaks—there's a big difference between blackened and burned. We recommend cooking to medium rather than well done—the longer you cook the meat, the dryer it will become.

NOTE: If you must use cold meat, you will have to adjust the cooking time and turn the steaks almost continuously to avoid burning.

If you want a low-fat dish, you'll be glad to know that blackening can be done without butter or oil. Simply omit the butter and use the same skillet you would if you were using butter.

Bronzed Pork Chops

MAKES **6** SERVINGS

Try bronzing your pork chops (or veal or lamb chops) when blackening outside is not possible. You can do bronzing indoors, so you don't have to worry about the weather and can enjoy this method any time.

2 ounces (½ stick) unsalted butter
6 (6-ounce) pork chops, about ¾
*   inch thick, at room temperature*
*   (see Note)*

*1 tablespoon **Chef Paul***
*   **Prudhomme's Pork and Veal***
*   **Magic** or **Chef Paul***
*   **Prudhomme's Meat Magic***

   Melt the butter in a pan or skillet large enough to hold the chops and set it aside.

   Heat a 10-inch skillet, preferably nonstick, over high heat to 350°, about 4 minutes.

   Be sure the meat is at room temperature (so the butter will adhere but not congeal). Dip the chops in the melted butter so that both sides are lightly and evenly coated. Place the meat on a plate and sprinkle (don't pour) ¼ teaspoon Pork and Veal (or Meat) Magic on one side of each chop. Carefully place the chops, two at a time, seasoned side down, in the skillet and reduce the heat to medium. Sprinkle ¼ teaspoon Pork and Veal Magic or Meat Magic on top of each chop. Cook, turning several times, to the desired doneness. Serve piping hot. Wipe out the skillet, bring it back to 350°, and repeat with the remaining chops. Serve immediately.

NOTE: If you must use cold meat, you will have to adjust the cooking time and turn the chops almost continuously to avoid burning.

If you want a low-fat dish, you'll be glad to know that bronzing can be done without butter or oil. Simply omit the butter and use the same skillet you would if you were using butter.

★

Bronzed Fish

MAKES **6** SERVINGS

Bronzing, which can be done indoors, is a versatile technique that works well on almost any firm-fleshed fish, so experiment with seasonings and cooking times and try it with several varieties, such as talapia, trout, redfish, red snapper, orange roughy, or tuna.

2 ounces (½ stick) unsalted butter
6 (4- to 5-ounce) fresh fish fillets,
   at room temperature
   (see Note)

1 tablespoon **Chef Paul Prudhomme's Blackened Redfish Magic** or **Chef Paul Prudhomme's Meat Magic**

Melt the butter in a pan or skillet large enough to hold one of the fillets and set it aside.

continued

Heat a 10-inch skillet, preferably nonstick, over high heat to 350°, about 4 minutes.

Be sure the fish is at room temperature (so the butter will adhere but not congeal). Dip the fillets in the melted butter so that both sides are lightly and evenly coated. Sprinkle (don't pour) ¼ teaspoon Blackened Redfish (or Meat) Magic on one side of each fillet. Carefully place the fillets, two at a time, in the skillet, seasoned side down. Sprinkle ¼ teaspoon of Blackened Redfish Magic on top of the fillets and reduce the heat to medium. Cook, turning several times, to the desired doneness. Be careful not to overcook or the fish will be too dry. Wipe out the skillet, bring it back to 350°, and repeat with the remaining fillets. Serve piping hot.

NOTE: If you must use cold fish, you will have to adjust the cooking time and turn the fillets almost continuously to avoid burning.

If you want a low-fat dish, you'll be glad to know that bronzing can be done without butter or oil. Simply omit the butter and use the same skillet you would if you were using butter.

SEE COLOR PHOTOGRAPH

Gone Fishing

Barbecued Shrimp

MAKES 2 SERVINGS

I want to warn you right now—this barbecue has absolutely no tomato in it. The shrimp are fun but messy to eat! In New Orleans most people wear bibs when they eat them because you peel your own shrimp and dip them in the sauce. And most of us soak up more sauce with our French bread.

2 dozen large shrimp with heads
    and shells, about 1 pound
    (see Note)
¼ pound (1 stick) plus 5
    tablespoons unsalted butter, in all
1½ teaspoons minced garlic
1 teaspoon Worcestershire sauce

1 tablespoon plus 1 teaspoon *Chef
    Paul Prudhomme's Seafood
    Magic or Chef Paul
    Prudhomme's Blackened
    Redfish Magic*
½ cup seafood stock (see page 194)
¼ cup beer, unopened but at room
    temperature

Rinse the shrimp in cold water and drain them well. Pinch off and discard the portion of the head from the eyes forward (including the eyes but not the protruding long spine above the eyes). Leave as much as possible of the orange-colored shrimp fat from the head attached to the body. Set aside.

Combine *1 stick* of the butter, the garlic, Worcestershire sauce, and Seafood Magic or Blackened Redfish Magic in a large skillet over high heat. When the butter melts, add the shrimp. Cook for 2 minutes, shaking (versus stirring) in a back-and-forth motion. Add the remaining 5 tablespoons butter and the stock. Cook and shake the pan for 2 minutes. Add the beer and cook and shake the pan for 1 minute more. Remove from the heat.

Serve immediately in bowls with lots of French bread on the side or on

continued

a platter with cooked rice mounded in the middle and the shrimp and sauce surrounding it.

NOTE: If you can't find shrimp with heads, go ahead and use headless shrimp. Your dish will still be great.

SEE COLOR PHOTOGRAPH

Garlic Shrimp and Oysters on Pasta

MAKES 2 SERVINGS

The sauce for this dish is best if made only two servings at a time. If you want to make more than two servings, do so in separate batches, but serve while piping hot.

2 quarts hot water
1 tablespoon salt
1 tablespoon vegetable oil
½ pound fresh spaghetti, or ⅓ pound dry
12 tablespoons (1½ sticks) unsalted butter, in all
½ cup chopped green onions
8 peeled medium shrimp, about 3 ounces

1 tablespoon minced garlic
1 tablespoon plus 1½ teaspoons **Chef Paul Prudhomme's Seafood Magic**
8 shucked medium oysters, drained, about 5 ounces
¾ cup warm seafood stock (see page 194)

Combine the hot water, salt, and oil in a large covered pot over high heat. When the water reaches a rolling boil, add the spaghetti, small amounts at a time, breaking up oil patches as you drop in the spaghetti. Return to boiling and cook, uncovered, to *al dente* stage (about 4 minutes if fresh, 7 minutes if dry), but do not overcook. During this cooking time, use a wooden or spaghetti spoon to lift the spaghetti out of the water by spoonfuls and shake strands back into the boiling water. It may be an old wives' tale, but this procedure seems to enhance the spaghetti's texture. Then immediately drain the spaghetti into a colander and stop its cooking by running cold water over it. (If you used dry spaghetti, first rinse with hot water to wash off the excess starch.) After the spaghetti has cooled thoroughly, about 2 to 3 minutes, pour about 1 tablespoon of vegetable oil in your hands and rub the spaghetti until it's well coated with oil. Set aside still in the colander.

Melt *6 tablespoons* of the butter in a large skillet over high heat, and add the green onions, shrimp, garlic, and Seafood Magic. Cook, vigorously shaking (not stirring) the pan in a back-and-forth motion, until the shrimp turn pink, about 1 minute. Add the oysters, stock, and the remaining 6 tablespoons butter. Cook, continuing to shake the pan, until the butter melts and the oysters curl, about 1 minute. Add the spaghetti, toss, and cook just until the spaghetti is heated through, about 1 minute. Remove from the heat and serve immediately.

For each serving, roll the spaghetti on a large fork and place on a serving plate. Top with the remaining sauce and garnish with the shrimp and oysters.

Shrimp or Crawfish Étouffée

MAKES 8 SERVINGS

★ ☆ ☆ ☆ ☆ ☆

Etouffée means "smothered," and in this traditional Louisiana dish the shrimp or crawfish are smothered with a great combination of seasoned vegetables in a dark roux. Use the shrimp or crawfish shells to make the stock. If you can't buy whole raw shrimp where you live, go ahead and use peeled ones and substitute vegetable stock for the seafood stock.

¼ cup chopped onions
¼ cup chopped celery
¼ cup chopped green bell peppers
7 tablespoons vegetable oil
¾ cup all-purpose flour
2 tablespoons **Chef Paul Prudhomme's Seafood Magic,** or 1 tablespoon **Chef Paul Prudhomme's Meat Magic** plus 1 tablespoon **Chef Paul Prudhomme's Poultry Magic,** in all

3 cups seafood stock, in all (see page 194)
½ pound (2 sticks) unsalted butter, in all
2 pounds uncooked whole medium shrimp or crawfish
1 cup very finely diced green onions
4 cups hot cooked white rice

Combine the onions, celery, and bell peppers in a bowl and set aside.

Heat the oil in a large, heavy skillet (preferably cast-iron) over high heat until it begins to smoke, about 4 minutes. Gradually whisk in the flour, stirring until smooth. Continue cooking, whisking constantly, until the roux is dark red-brown, about 3 to 5 minutes, being careful not to let it scorch or splash on your skin. Remove from the heat and immediately stir in the vegetables and *1 tablespoon* of the Seafood Magic (or other Magic Seasoning) with a wooden spoon. Continue stirring until cool, about 5 minutes.

Bring *2 cups* of the stock to a boil in a 2-quart saucepan over high heat. Add the roux by spoonfuls to the boiling stock, stirring until dissolved between each addition. Reduce the heat to low and cook, whisking almost constantly, until the flour taste is gone, about 2 minutes. If any of the mixture begins to stick to the pan bottom and burn, don't continue to scrape that part of the pan bottom. Remove from the heat and set aside.

Melt *1 stick* of the butter in a 4-quart saucepan over medium heat. Stir in the crawfish or shrimp and the green onions and sauté, stirring almost constantly, for 1 minute. Add the remaining butter, the stock mixture, and the remaining 1 cup stock. Cook, constantly shaking (versus stirring) the pan in a back-and-forth motion, until the butter melts and is mixed into the sauce, about 4 to 6 minutes. Add the remaining Seafood Magic (or other Magic Seasoning), stir well, and remove from the heat. If the sauce starts to separate, add 2 tablespoons more stock or water and shake the pan until it combines. Serve immediately over the rice.

Shrimp Creole

The distinctive taste of this traditional dish comes from the fat in the shrimp heads, the fresh tomatoes, the caramelized onions, and the butter. The sauce is best if made the day before serving—make the seafood stock first, then the sauce. When ready to serve, skim off the oil from the surface and reheat the sauce to a boil. Reduce the heat to very low, add the raw, peeled fresh shrimp, cover, and cook just until the shrimp turn pink, about 5 minutes. This dish is well seasoned as is, but if you like a little more heat, you may want to offer Magic Pepper Sauce as a condiment.

3½ pounds large shrimp with heads and shells, as fatty as possible (see Note)

¼ cup chicken fat, pork lard, beef fat, butter, or oil

2½ cups finely diced onions, in all

1¾ cups finely diced celery

1½ cups finely diced green bell peppers

4 tablespoons unsalted butter

2 teaspoons minced fresh garlic

1 bay leaf

3 tablespoons **Chef Paul Prudhomme's Seafood Magic** or **Chef Paul Prudhomme's Poultry Magic**

1½ teaspoons **Chef Paul Prudhomme's Magic Pepper Sauce**

1½ cups seafood stock, in all *(see page 194)*

3 cups finely chopped peeled *(see page 3)* tomatoes (preferably Creole)

1½ cups tomato sauce

2 teaspoons sugar

5 cups hot cooked white rice

Rinse, peel, and refrigerate the shrimp until needed. Use the heads and shells to make the stock.

Heat the chicken or other fat in a 4-quart saucepan over high heat until melted. Add *1 cup* of the onions and cook, stirring frequently, for 3 minutes. Reduce the heat to medium-low and continue to cook, stirring frequently, until the onions are a rich brown color but not burned, about 3 to 5 minutes. Add the remaining onions, the celery, bell peppers, and butter.

Raise the heat to high and cook, stirring occasionally, until the peppers and celery start to get tender, about 5 minutes. Add the garlic, bay leaf, and Seafood Magic (or Poultry Magic). Stir well, then add the Magic Pepper Sauce and *½ cup* of the stock. Reduce the heat to medium and cook, stirring occasionally and scraping the pan bottom well, for 5 minutes to allow the seasonings to marry and the vegetables to brown further.

Add the tomatoes, reduce the heat to low, and simmer, stirring occasionally and scraping the pan bottom, for 10 minutes. Stir in the tomato sauce and simmer, stirring occasionally, for 5 minutes. Add the remaining stock and the sugar, and continue simmering, stirring occasionally, for 15 minutes.

Cool and refrigerate if making the day before serving.

If serving immediately, remove from the heat and add the shrimp. Cover and let sit until the shrimp are plump and pink, about 5 to 10 minutes. Serve over the rice.

NOTE: The shrimp fat is the orange-colored substance in the heads. If shrimp with heads are not available, buy 2 pounds of shrimp without heads but with shells for making the stock.

Lotsa
Crab Crab Cakes

MAKES 10 TO 12 CRAB CAKES, ENOUGH FOR 5 OR 6 MAIN-DISH
SERVINGS OR 10 TO 12 APPETIZER SERVINGS

★ ☆ ☆ ☆ ☆ ☆

When I order crab cakes in a restaurant, I like lotsa crab, notta lotta bread crumbs. That's the way these crab cakes are made, with just enough crumbs to hold the other ingredients together. They are juicy and spicy, and the rich cream sauce is a perfect complement.

CRAB CAKES

5 cups soft bread crumbs, in all *(use fresh bread—French preferably— and grate or use a food processor)*
7 tablespoons unsalted butter
2 cups chopped onions
1 cup chopped green bell peppers
1 cup chopped celery
3 tablespoons plus 2 teaspoons **Chef Paul Prudhomme's Seafood Magic**, in all
1 cup chopped fresh parsley, in all
1 tablespoon Worcestershire sauce
1 teaspoon **Chef Paul Prudhomme's Magic Pepper Sauce**, optional

1 teaspoon minced fresh garlic
½ cup seafood stock *(see page 194)* or bottled clam juice
1 pound lump crabmeat, picked over for shell and cartilage
3 eggs, lightly beaten
1 cup heavy cream
1 cup vegetable oil

•

SAUCE

2 cups heavy cream, in all
½ cup chopped green onion tops

To make the crab cakes, toast *3 cups* of the bread crumbs in a 12-inch skillet over high heat, shaking the skillet occasionally, until the crumbs are light brown, about 5 to 6 minutes. (The volume of the crumbs will be reduced to about 2¼ cups.) Remove from the heat and set aside.

Return the skillet to high heat and add the butter, onions, bell peppers, and celery. Cook, stirring once or twice, until the vegetables start to brown, about 6 minutes. Stir in *2 tablespoons* of the Seafood Magic, *½ cup* of the parsley, the Worcestershire sauce, Magic Pepper Sauce, and garlic, and cook over high heat until the mixture sticks to the bottom of the pan, about 5 minutes. Add the stock or clam juice, scrape up the crust on the bottom of the skillet, and remove from the heat.

Place the toasted bread crumbs in a medium-size mixing bowl. Add the crabmeat, the remaining Seafood Magic and parsley, the vegetable mixture from the skillet, the eggs and cream, and stir gently without breaking up the lumps of crabmeat. Remove ½ cup of the mixture and set it aside to use in the sauce. Refrigerate the remaining mixture for 1½ hours.

Meanwhile, to make the sauce, combine *1 cup* of the cream and the reserved ½ cup crab mixture in an 8-inch skillet over high heat. Cook, stirring constantly, for 3 minutes. Stir in the remaining 1 cup of cream and cook 2 minutes. Add the green onion tops and bring the sauce to a boil, stirring occasionally, about 2 minutes. Remove from the heat but keep warm.

To finish the dish, remove the crab mixture from the refrigerator.

Heat the oil in a 10-inch skillet over high heat to 260°, using a cooking thermometer or electric skillet. While the oil is heating, place the remaining 2 cups of bread crumbs in a bowl. Measure ½ cup of the crabmeat mixture and form it into a round cake about 3 inches in diameter, and dredge it in the crumbs to coat it completely. Repeat with the remaining mixture to form the rest of the crab cakes. Be careful not to make the cakes too flat, or they might break when you turn them over.

continued

When the oil reaches 260°, add 4 of the crab cakes to the skillet and fry them until brown, about 3 minutes on each side. Drain on paper towels and repeat until all the crab cakes are fried.

To serve as an appetizer, pour a generous ¼ cup of the sauce onto each plate and top with a crab cake. For a main course, allow ½ cup sauce and 2 crab cakes.

SEE COLOR PHOTOGRAPH

Piquant Crabmeat Ramekins

MAKES **8** APPETIZER SERVINGS

Here is a tasty little appetizer that you serve in, and eat from, the ramekin. This elegant dish is incredibly easy to make. And do take the bit of time it takes to make your own mayonnaise. It's so much better than the commercial product, and you'll find you have lots of uses for the remainder.

2½ tablespoons unsalted butter

⅓ cup finely diced onions

⅓ cup finely diced celery

⅓ cup finely diced green bell
  peppers

¼ cup finely diced green onions

½ teaspoon minced garlic

6 tablespoons Homemade
  Mayonnaise, in all *(see page 193)*

4 teaspoons Creole (preferred) or
  brown mustard

2 teaspoons minced fresh parsley

2 teaspoons Worcestershire sauce

1 teaspoon salt

1 teaspoon cayenne

1 teaspoon **Chef Paul
  Prudhomme's Magic Pepper
  Sauce**

½ teaspoon black pepper

½ teaspoon white pepper

1 egg

1 pound lump crabmeat, picked
  over for shell and cartilage

½ cup heavy cream

Paprika

Melt the butter in a 1-quart pot and add the onions, celery, bell peppers, green onions, and garlic. Sauté over high heat, stirring occasionally, until the vegetables are tender but still firm, about 5 minutes. Remove from the heat. Stir in *2½ tablespoons* of the mayonnaise, the mustard, parsley, Worcestershire, salt, cayenne, Magic Pepper Sauce, and black and white peppers.

Preheat the oven to 350°.

Beat the egg into the vegetable mixture with a whisk. Add the crabmeat and toss gently, leaving lumps intact as much as possible. Spoon into eight ½-cup ovenproof ramekins. Pour *1 tablespoon* cream over the top of each, then spread a thin, even layer of the remaining mayonnaise on top and sprinkle with paprika. Bake until brown and bubbly, about 15 to 18 minutes. Serve immediately.

Broiled Flounder

Flounder is not only popular but versatile. Although it usually appears on restaurant menus stuffed, we thought you'd like to try broiling. In our version the fish is actually cooked in a liquid, a little like poaching. It's a method that keeps the fish moist and highlights its delicate flavor, which stuffing sometimes overpowers. You can use this recipe with other kinds of fish, such as trout, sole, bass, red snapper, redfish, tilefish, drum, or walleye. And you can substitute white wine for the lemon juice for a different taste.

2 tablespoons unsalted butter or margarine
2 tablespoons freshly squeezed lemon juice

*1 tablespoon plus ½ teaspoon **Chef Paul Prudhomme's Seafood Magic**, in all*
4 (4- to 5-ounce) flounder fillets, about ½ inch thick

Position the top rack of the broiler about 5 inches from the heat source and preheat the broiler.

Pour enough water into a 9×12-inch baking pan to measure ¼ inch deep. Add the butter or margarine, lemon juice, and 1½ teaspoons of the Seafood Magic. Place the pan under the broiler for 5 minutes to heat the liquid.

Meanwhile, evenly sprinkle one side of each fillet with ½ teaspoon Seafood Magic. Lay the fillets, seasoned side up, in the pan and broil until lightly browned on top, 5 minutes if your fillets are exactly ½ inch thick. Remove with a slotted spatula, draining off all excess liquid, and serve immediately.

Friday Night Fish Fry

Fried fish for supper on Friday nights is a tradition in many parts of the country, and this recipe makes it simple to prepare. One secret to really good fried fish is not to crowd the skillet. The fish should always touch the bottom of the pan, so fry it in batches if necessary. You can use this recipe for many kinds of fish, such as trout, perch, flounder, grouper, or orange roughy.

1½ cups all-purpose flour
*1 tablespoon **Chef Paul***
  Prudhomme's Seafood Magic
1 egg, beaten

1 cup milk
6 (4-ounce) fresh fish fillets, about
  ½ inch thick
Vegetable oil for frying

Combine the flour and 1½ teaspoons of the Seafood Magic in a shallow pan (cake or pie pans work well), and in a separate shallow pan, combine the egg and milk until well blended. Sprinkle each fillet with ¼ teaspoon of Seafood Magic.

Pour enough oil into a large skillet to measure ¼ inch deep and heat it to about 350°, about 4 to 5 minutes. Use either an electric skillet or a cooking thermometer and adjust the heat as necessary to maintain the oil's temperature.

Dredge each fillet in the seasoned flour, shake off the excess, and coat well with the milk mixture. Just before frying, drain off the egg mixture and dredge the fillets once more in the flour, shaking off the excess. Fry the fish in the hot oil until golden brown, about 1 to 2 minutes per side. Drain on paper towels and serve immediately.

Oven-Fried Catfish

★☆★☆★☆★☆★☆

You may have a hard time believing that something that tastes this great can be healthful, but it is because it's cooked with almost no oil. Don't substitute or leave out the fresh parsley and green onions because their flavors are very important to the end result. If fresh catfish isn't available, this recipe works just as well with any type of fish fillet. Always look for the freshest local products—they will always have the best flavor. If you follow this recipe exactly, you'll be rewarded by a crispy texture and juicy fish.

4 (4- to 5-ounce) fresh catfish
  fillets
2 tablespoons plus 2 teaspoons
  **Chef Paul Prudhomme's
  Seafood Magic** (preferred) or
  **Chef Paul Prudhomme's Meat
  Magic** or **Chef Paul
  Prudhomme's Vegetable Magic,**
  in all

½ cup toasted bread crumbs
2 tablespoons finely chopped fresh
  parsley
3 tablespoons finely sliced green
  onions
1 tablespoon olive oil

Sprinkle all surfaces of the fish evenly with *1 tablespoon plus 2 teaspoons* of the Seafood Magic (or other Magic Seasoning) and gently rub it in.
  Preheat the oven to 450°.
  Combine the bread crumbs, parsley, green onions, and remaining Sea-

food Magic (or other Magic Seasoning) in a bowl. Add the oil and combine it until the crumbs are moist.

Dredge the fillets, one at a time, in the bread crumb mixture, pressing down gently on each side. Shake off any excess crumbs. Place the seasoned fish on a nonstick baking sheet, presentation side up, and cook for 6 minutes. Turn the fish over and cook for 6 minutes. Turn over one more time (presentation side up) and cook until done, about 4 minutes more. Serve immediately.

Napa Valley Fish

MAKES **6** SERVINGS

Although the alcohol is burned off during cooking, marinating the fish in wine gives it a unique delicate flavor. We've discovered a great way to turn fish over when grilling without its breaking up. We use a pair of wire screens, the kind made to cover a skillet and prevent grease from splattering. Place one screen between the grill and the fish and the other on top of the fish. When you're ready to turn the fish, just hold it firmly between the screens and flip. You can probably find the screens in the kitchen gadget section of your supermarket.

Smoking chips, optional
6 (8- to 10-ounce) firm-fleshed fish
  fillets, such as talapia, catfish,
  pompano, red snapper, or salmon
  or tuna steaks, about ½ inch
  thick

1 cup white wine, such as
  chardonnay or sauvignon blanc
2 tablespoons **Chef Paul**
  Prudhomme's Seafood Magic *or*
  Chef Paul Prudhomme's
  Blackened Redfish Magic

If using smoking chips, soak according to package directions.

Place the fish in a glass or plastic container, pour the wine over it, and let sit for at least 15 minutes or up to an hour. Light a charcoal or gas grill, and when the coals are coated with white ash, add the smoking chips if desired.

Remove the fish from the wine and drain off the excess. Sprinkle ½ teaspoon Seafood Magic or Blackened Redfish Magic evenly on each side of all the fillets and gently pat it in. When the fire dies down, grill the fish for 3 minutes on one side, then turn it over and grill until done to your liking—the time will depend upon the variety of fish and the heat of the grill. You can check doneness by cutting through one fillet—if done, it will be opaque all the way through. Serve immediately.

★

Magic Grilled Fish

MAKES **6** SERVINGS

Don't be afraid to cook directly in flames. If you watch the timing carefully, the fish won't burn, and the seared Blackened Redfish Magic will give the fish a taste you won't forget! You can use this recipe with just about any firm-fleshed fish, such as redfish, pompano, tilefish, golden tile, red snapper, walleyed pike or sac-a-lait, or salmon or tuna steaks, as long as they're ½ inch thick. And while you have the fire going, grill an assortment of fresh vegetables to complete the meal.

continued

6 (8- to 10-ounce) fish fillets or
   steaks, about ½ inch thick
¾ cup (1½ sticks) unsalted butter
   or margarine, melted

4 tablespoons **Chef Paul
   Prudhomme's Blackened
   Redfish Magic** or **Chef Paul
   Prudhomme's Seafood Magic**

Heat the grill as hot as possible, with flames reaching above the grates, before putting the fish on the grill. If you have them, add dried wood chunks to the glowing coals to make the fire even hotter.

Dip each fillet in the melted butter so that both sides are well coated. Drain off the excess, then sprinkle each side of each fillet evenly with 1 teaspoon Blackened Redfish Magic or Seafood Magic and pat it in. Place the fish directly over the flames and pour 1 teaspoon melted butter over each fillet. Be careful—the butter may flame up. Cook, uncovered, directly in the flames until the underside is well browned, about 2 minutes. The time will vary according to the thickness of the fish and the heat of the grill. Turn the fillets over and grill until cooked through, about 2 minutes more. Serve immediately.

Bird Is the Word

Magic Chicken Pasta

MAKES 4 SERVINGS

Although this dish is so quick that you can whip it up after you get in from work, it's also so elegant that you could invite company and they'd think you came home in the middle of the afternoon to prepare it! Serve with a crisp green salad and bread hot from the oven, and your reputation will be made.

4 cups cooked pasta (about 3 cups before cooking)

8 ounces diced chicken breast

*1 tablespoon plus 1 teaspoon **Chef Paul Prudhomme's Poultry Magic**, in all*

4 tablespoons unsalted butter

6 tablespoons thinly sliced green onions

2 cups heavy cream

Cook the pasta according to package directions, drain, and set aside.

Sprinkle the chicken with *1 teaspoon* Poultry Magic and rub it in well.

Melt the butter in a 12-inch skillet over high heat, shaking the skillet once or twice. When the butter sizzles, in about 2 minutes, add the chicken and remaining 1 tablespoon of Poultry Magic, and cook for 3 minutes, stirring occasionally. Add the onions and cream and bring to a boil. Cook, occasionally whisking gently, until the cream begins to thicken, about 5 minutes. Add the pasta, return to a boil, and remove from the heat.

Buffalo Chicken Wings

MAKES 16 APPETIZER SERVINGS, 3 PIECES TO A SERVING

These may have been the trendy appetizer of the early '90s, but they're still delicious! I have seen Buffalo Wings on menus all over the world, and I'd be willing to bet my fillet knife this recipe will be around for many a year to come.

24 chicken wings (see Note)
10 tablespoons (1¼) sticks
    unsalted butter, in all
1 tablespoon cayenne, in all

3 tablespoons **Chef Paul**
    Prudhomme's Poultry Magic,
    in all
2 cups vegetable oil

Remove the chicken wings from the refrigerator and let them come to room temperature. If they're cold, the butter will congeal and won't coat the wings evenly.

Melt *5 tablespoons* of the butter with *1½ teaspoons* of the cayenne in a small saucepan over medium heat. Remove from the heat and let cool slightly.

Cut the chicken wings into 3 parts at the joints. Discard the tips or use them for another purpose, such as making stock. This will leave 2 meaty parts per wing for this recipe.

Place the wing pieces in a medium mixing bowl, sprinkle with *2 tablespoons* of the Poultry Magic, and add the butter/cayenne mixture. Work the butter and seasonings into the wing pieces, distributing the seasonings as evenly as possible.

Heat the oil in a large skillet over high heat to 375°, using a cooking thermometer or an electric skillet to be sure the oil's temperature is maintained. When the oil reaches 375°, add as many wing pieces as will fit easily in a single layer. Fry until they are brown, about 4 to 6 minutes. Drain on paper towels and repeat with the remaining chicken.

Meanwhile, melt the remaining 5 tablespoons of butter in a small skillet over low heat. Add the remaining Poultry Magic and cayenne, cook until the butter starts to brown, then remove from the heat. When all the wing pieces are cooked, put them in a bowl and pour the hot seasoned butter over them, then toss until the chicken is coated.

Serve immediately with blue cheese dressing, Chef Paul Prudhomme's Magic Pepper Sauce, and celery sticks.

N o t e: Some stores now sell chicken wing "drumettes," already cut to make this and similar recipes. If you use drumettes, you'll need 48 of them.

Broiled Honey Chicken Wings

MAKES 8 APPETIZER SERVINGS, 2 PIECES TO A SERVING

This chicken wing appetizer is completely different from Buffalo Chicken Wings, both in seasoning and method of preparation. To tell you the truth, it's hard to decide which one I like better. Maybe I'd better try both recipes again. . . .

continued

SEASONING MIX

2 tablespoons *Chef Paul Prudhomme's Meat Magic*
1½ teaspoons ground ginger
1 teaspoon ground California Beauty chile peppers (see page 2)
½ teaspoon rubbed sage
¼ teaspoon ground cumin

8 chicken wings (see Note)
4 tablespoons unsalted butter
½ cup chopped onions
2 teaspoons minced fresh garlic
½ cup dry sherry
2 tablespoons soy sauce
½ cup chicken stock (see page 196)
½ cup honey

•

If your broiler is electric, preheat it.

Cut the chicken wings into 3 parts at the joints. Discard the tips or use them for another purpose, such as making stock. This will leave 2 meaty parts per wing for this recipe.

Combine the seasoning mix ingredients in a small bowl. Sprinkle *1 tablespoon* of the seasoning mix over the wing pieces and rub it in well.

Melt the butter in a heavy 12-inch skillet over high heat. When the butter sizzles, add the wing pieces and brown them on one side. Turn them over, add the onions and garlic, and cook, occasionally scraping the pan, until the chicken is browned on the other side, about 10 to 12 minutes in all. Add the sherry, soy sauce, stock, and remaining seasoning mix, stir, and bring to a full boil. Remove from the heat, add the honey, and let sit for 3 minutes.

If you're using a gas broiler, turn it on now. With tongs, remove the wings from the sauce and place them on the broiler pan in a single layer. Broil, turning once, until they are browned and crisp, about 2 minutes on each side. Pour the sauce into a bowl for dipping, and serve with the wings immediately.

NOTE: Some stores now sell chicken wing "drumettes," already cut to make this and similar recipes. If you use drumettes, you'll need 16 of them.

Left to right: Corn Chowder (page 12), Black Bean Soup
(page 16), Milwaukee Potato Soup (page 14)

Eye-Opener Omelet (page 32)

✩

Barbecued Shrimp (page 71)

Bronzed Fish (page 67)

★

Brisket Barbecue (page 152)
with Big Bang Barbecue Sauce (page 186)
and Bobby Prudhomme's Macaroni Salad (page 176)

★

Chef Paul's Favorite Meal:
Roasted Pork with Gingersnap Gravy (page 132),
Traditional Potato Salad (page 173),
Dirty Rice (page 52), and Candied Yams (page 175)

☆

Lotsa Crab Crab Cakes (page 78)

Flank and Greens (page 146)

★

Sticky Chicken (page 108)
with Corn Maque Choux (page 168)

Chicken Florentine (page 95)

☆

Lentils and Rice (page 48)

Monday Red Beans (page 53)

Chicken Florentine

I'll let the historians worry about how this dish got its famous Italian name. What's important to me—and to you too, I'll bet—is its exciting taste and texture.

SEASONING MIX
2 tablespoons plus 2 teaspoons
   Chef Paul Prudhomme's
   Poultry Magic
½ teaspoon ground nutmeg

•

8 boneless, skinless chicken breasts
½ cup all-purpose flour
3 eggs

¼ cup plus 3 tablespoons half-and-
   half, in all
¼ cup bread crumbs
½ cup grated Parmesan cheese,
   in all
8 tablespoons (1 stick) unsalted
   butter, in all
1½ pounds rinsed fresh spinach
   (preferred) or thawed frozen
   spinach, drained and toweled dry

Combine the seasoning mix ingredients in a small bowl.

Place the chicken breasts on a flat surface and pound them a few times with the flat side of a cleaver or heavy knife. Sprinkle the breasts with *1 tablespoon* of the seasoning mix and rub it in well.

Combine the flour and *1 teaspoon* of the seasoning mix in a shallow dish. Combine the eggs, *3 tablespoons* of the half-and-half, and ¼ *teaspoon* of the seasoning mix in another shallow dish. Beat thoroughly with a fork. Combine the bread crumbs, *1 teaspoon* of the seasoning mix, and ¼ *cup* of the Parmesan cheese in a third dish.

continued

Dredge the chicken breasts one at a time in the seasoned flour, dip them in the egg mixture, and then dredge them in the bread crumb mixture, shaking off any excess crumbs. Add the remaining ¼ cup half-and-half to the egg mixture, beat briefly with a fork, and set aside.

Melt *4 tablespoons* (½ stick) of the butter in a 12-inch skillet over high heat. As soon as the butter starts to sizzle, add the chicken breasts and brown them on both sides. Remove the chicken from the skillet and set aside. Add the remaining butter and the remaining seasoning mix to the pan. When the butter sizzles, add the spinach, gently pressing it down, and cook until it starts to wilt, about 1 minute. Pour the reserved egg/half-and-half mixture over the spinach and stir well. Sprinkle with the remaining ¼ cup Parmesan cheese. Place the chicken breasts on top, cover, and reduce the heat to medium-low. Cook until the chicken is cooked through, about 13 minutes.

SEE COLOR PHOTOGRAPH

Chicken à la King

MAKES **4** TO **6** SERVINGS

This recipe takes the traditional approach to the dish—rich and creamy, spiked with a bit of sherry. Colorful and delicious, it's just perfect when you want a very special meal. Serve in pastry shells or crêpes or over rice, pasta, or croissants.

3 tablespoons plus 1 teaspoon *Chef*
Paul Prudhomme's Poultry
Magic

1¼ teaspoons dry mustard

¾ teaspoon ground savory

½ teaspoon ground nutmeg

•

2 pounds boneless, skinless chicken
breasts, cut into 1-inch cubes

8 tablespoons (1 stick) unsalted
butter, softened

5 tablespoons unsalted butter, cut
into pats

¼ cup all-purpose flour

¼ cup plus 2 tablespoons dry
sherry, in all

1 cup chopped onions

1 cup chopped green bell peppers

1 cup chopped red bell peppers

1 cup chopped yellow bell peppers

2 cups thinly sliced fresh
mushrooms

2½ cups heavy cream, in all

Combine the seasoning mix ingredients in a small bowl. Sprinkle *2 table-spoons* of the seasoning mix over the chicken and rub it in well. Set aside.

Combine the stick of softened butter with the flour until completely blended. Set aside.

Preheat a 5-quart pot over high heat for 4 minutes. Add the chicken and dot the pats of butter evenly over the chicken. Cover the pot and cook without stirring until the chicken can easily be unstuck from the bottom of the pot, about 5 to 6 minutes. Stir in *¼ cup* of the sherry, the onions, peppers, mushrooms, and remaining seasoning mix. Cover and cook for 5 minutes. Add the butter/flour mix a spoonful at a time, stirring constantly as the mixture dissolves and the sauce thickens. Stir in *2 cups* of the cream and heat until small "volcanoes" begin to erupt in the sauce, but do not allow the sauce to come to a rolling boil. Let the volcanoes erupt 3 times, stirring after each eruption. Add the remaining ½ cup cream and heat until another group of small volcanoes erupts, about 1 minute. Remove from the heat and stir in the remaining sherry.

Louisiana
Chicken and Dumplings

MAKES **8** SERVINGS

This is a real down-home dish, the kind of food you fix for a large family. It's sure to bring back memories for anyone who ever lived in a small town or visited relatives in the country. Because it's in several parts, the recipe looks complicated, but just take it one step at a time and it will all come together.

SEASONING MIX
3 tablespoons **Chef Paul Prudhomme's Poultry Magic**
½ teaspoon gumbo filé (filé powder or ground sassafras), optional

•

2 (2½- to 3-pound) chicken fryers, all visible fat removed, each cut into 8 pieces

1 cup all-purpose flour
Vegetable oil for frying
Dumplings (recipe follows)
2 quarts chicken stock (see page 196)
3 cups chopped onions
3 cups chopped green bell peppers
2 cups heavy cream
2 tablespoons unsalted butter, melted

If using the gumbo filé, combine it with the Poultry Magic in a small bowl to make the seasoning mix.

Sprinkle the chicken evenly with *1 tablespoon plus 1 teaspoon* of the seasoning mix (or Poultry Magic alone) and rub it in well.

Combine *1 tablespoon* of the seasoning with the flour in a paper or plastic bag. Place the chicken pieces in the bag and shake to coat, reserving the leftover flour mixture for the roux.

Heat 1 inch of oil in a very large skillet over medium heat to 230° to 250° and cook the chicken in batches, large pieces and skin side down first. An electric skillet works well for this because the temperature is automatically maintained; if you're not using an electric skillet, adjust the heat to maintain the oil's temperature. Cook until golden brown on both sides, about 30 minutes, and drain on paper towels.

Meanwhile, make the dumpling dough and set aside.

Combine the stock, onions, bell peppers, cream, and remaining seasoning in a 6-quart pot over high heat and bring to a boil. Reduce the heat and simmer, stirring occasionally, until the bell peppers darken in color, about 5 minutes. Add the chicken and continue simmering, stirring occasionally, until the chicken is tender, about 20 minutes.

Meanwhile, cook the dumplings by dropping the batter by teaspoonfuls onto a rack in a steamer and steaming until cooked through, about 5 to 7 minutes. If you don't have a steamer, use a colander over a small amount of water in a large saucepan and cover with a lid or aluminum foil.

To thicken the sauce, make a roux by stirring together the melted butter and 2 tablespoons of the reserved seasoned flour. Stir in ½ cup of liquid from the chicken pot and return this to the pot. Cover and simmer for 2 minutes. Add the dumplings and stir gently. Cook until the dumplings are heated through, about 2 minutes.

To serve, place 2 pieces of chicken and 5 dumplings on each plate. Top with ½ cup sauce. (Any leftover sauce is great taken out on the back porch and eaten as soup.)

Dumplings

4 eggs

½ cup minced onions

2 teaspoons baking powder

1 tablespoon **Chef Paul Prudhomme's Vegetable Magic**

½ teaspoon ground nutmeg

½ teaspoon rubbed sage

½ cup milk

¼ pound (1 stick) unsalted butter, melted

2½ cups all-purpose flour

continued

Combine the eggs and onions in a large bowl and beat vigorously with a whisk until frothy, about 2 minutes. Add the baking powder (break up any lumps) and seasonings, and whisk until blended. Stir in the milk and butter. Gradually add the flour, a third at a time, to the center of the mixture, beating well after each addition. Cook as directed above.

★

Chicken Pot Pie

MAKES **8** SERVINGS

The corn in the filling of this rich, flavorful pot pie complements the chicken and other vegetables and emphasizes the flavor of the cornmeal in the crust. And the dish is as beautiful to look at as it is to taste. That's because our delicious crust works almost like children's clay before baking, which means you can shape it just about any way you want. Crimp or scallop the edges or experiment with decorative cutout shapes.

SEASONING MIX

2 tablespoons plus 2 teaspoons
  Chef Paul Prudhomme's
  Poultry Magic
½ teaspoon ground cardamom

•

DOUGH

2 cups all-purpose flour
¾ cup toasted cornmeal (see Note)
2 teaspoons seasoning mix
½ pound (2 sticks) unsalted butter,
  cut into pats
½ cup chilled chicken stock
  (see page 2)

•

FILLING

2 tablespoons plus ½ teaspoon
  seasoning mix

2 pounds boneless, skinless chicken
  breasts
8 slices bacon, diced
2 cups chopped onions
1½ cups chopped celery
1 cup chopped green bell peppers
1 cup fresh corn kernels (about
  2 ears)
4 cups chicken stock, in all
  (see page 196)
3 cloves
¼ cup toasted cornmeal (see Note)
1 cup tiny pearl onions, peeled
3 tablespoons chopped fresh parsley
2 cups sliced carrots

•

All-purpose flour
Vegetable oil cooking spray

Combine the seasoning mix ingredients in a small bowl.

TO MAKE THE DOUGH: Combine the flour, ¾ cup toasted cornmeal, and seasoning mix in the bowl of a food processor and pulse until blended, about 5 or 6 times. Distribute the butter over the dry ingredients and process until blended, 25 to 30 seconds. With the machine running, add the chilled stock in a thin stream and process until thoroughly blended, about 40 seconds. Form the dough into a ball and refrigerate for at least 30 minutes.

continued

TO MAKE THE FILLING: Sprinkle *2 teaspoons* of the seasoning mix evenly over the chicken and rub it in well.

Fry the bacon in a 12-inch skillet over high heat until crisp, about 8 to 9 minutes. Remove with a slotted spoon and drain on paper towels.

Heat the bacon fat remaining in the skillet over high heat and add the chicken. Fry, turning several times, until lightly browned, about 7 to 10 minutes. Remove the chicken to a bowl.

Add the chopped onions, celery, bell peppers, corn, and *1 tablespoon* of the seasoning mix to the fat in the skillet. Cook, scraping the bottom of the skillet occasionally as the mixture forms crusts, about 5 minutes. Pour any chicken juices that have accumulated in the bowl, plus *½ cup* of the stock, into the skillet and scrape up any crust on the bottom. Add the cloves and simmer until the mixture begins to stick again, about 6 minutes. Add another *½ cup* stock, scrape the bottom of the skillet, and simmer until most of the liquid has evaporated, about 6 to 8 minutes. Stir in the toasted cornmeal and cook until the cornmeal sticks hard to the bottom of the skillet but is not burning, about 2 to 3 minutes. Add *1 cup* more stock, scrape the bottom of the skillet, and bring the mixture to a simmer. Add the pearl onions, parsley, carrots, reserved fried bacon, remaining 2 cups of stock, and remaining seasoning mix. Scrape the bottom and sides of the skillet and bring to a boil, reduce the heat to low and simmer until the mixture thickens somewhat and the vegetables are barely tender, about 8 to 10 minutes. Remove from the heat.

Dice the cooled chicken breasts into ½-inch pieces. Stir the chicken into the skillet and pour the mixture into a shallow pan. Refrigerate about 30 minutes.

TO FINISH: Preheat the oven to 350°.

Carefully divide the dough in half with the side of your hand. Sprinkle a clean surface lightly with flour. Flatten one piece of the dough with your hand and roll it out to a circle about ⅛ inch thick. Repeat with the other half of the dough. Coat a deep pie or cake pan (it fits perfectly into a 9-inch round pan that is 3 inches high) with cooking spray and line with one piece of the rolled-out dough.

Fill the lined pan with the cooled mixture and cover with the second round of dough. Seal the edges with the tines of a fork and pierce the center of the top of the crust. Bake until golden brown, 50 minutes to 1 hour. Cool 15 to 20 minutes before cutting into wedges to serve.

NOTE: To toast the total amount of cornmeal you need for this recipe, place 1 cup in a small skillet over medium-high heat. Shake the pan and flip the cornmeal constantly until it turns a light golden brown, about 4 minutes. Remove from the heat so it doesn't continue cooking. If you're using a cast-iron skillet, you may have to transfer it to another container to stop the browning.

★

Chicken Fricassee

MAKES **4** SERVINGS

Fricassee means different things to different people, but the term simply means any meat that is cut up and served in its own gravy. When most Americans hear "fricassee," they think of chicken, so that's the recipe I've selected for you.

continued

SEASONING MIX

4 tablespoons *Chef Paul*
  Prudhomme's Meat Magic

2 teaspoons paprika

1 teaspoon dry mustard

¼ teaspoon ground allspice

•

1 (3½- to 4-pound) chicken, all
  visible fat removed, cut into 8
  pieces

2 tablespoons olive oil

½ cup chopped onions

½ cup chopped celery

1 cup sliced carrots, in all

3 small bay leaves

1 cup peeled tiny fresh pearl onions

1½ cups small fresh mushrooms

1 teaspoon minced fresh garlic

¼ cup all-purpose flour

2 cups chicken stock (see page 196)

1 cup heavy cream

Hot cooked egg noodles

Combine the seasoning mix ingredients in a small bowl.

Sprinkle *2 tablespoons* of the seasoning mix over the chicken and rub it in well.

Preheat a heavy 5-quart pot, preferably nonstick, over high heat for 4 minutes. Add the olive oil and the chicken, skin side down. Cook, turning several times, until the chicken is deep brown on all sides. You may have to cook the chicken in batches. Remove the chicken to a bowl and set it aside.

To the drippings in the pot, add the chopped onions, celery, *½ cup* of the carrots, bay leaves, and *2 tablespoons* of the seasoning mix. Cook, scraping the bottom of the pot occasionally, until the vegetables turn golden brown, about 3 to 4 minutes. Stir in the pearl onions, mushrooms, garlic, remaining seasoning mix, and flour, and cook, scraping constantly to keep the mixture from sticking, about 1 to 2 minutes. Stir in the stock and remaining carrots and bring to a boil. Return the chicken and any accumulated juices to the pot and bring the mixture back to a boil. Cook 5 minutes, stir in the cream, and reduce the heat to low. Cover and simmer until the chicken is tender, about 12 to 15 minutes.

Serve over the noodles.

Chicken Mole Tostadas

There is a mystery in this very traditional Mexican dish, but it's not in the title. The word *mole* just means "sauce," and *tostadas* means "toasted"—chicken in sauce with toasted tortillas. The secret is the presence of chocolate and peanut butter in the sauce, but with all the spicy ingredients, they only enrich the sauce rather than stand out.

SEASONING MIX

2 tablespoons plus 1 teaspoon
ground dried New Mexico chile
peppers (see Note 1)

2 tablespoons ground dried guajillo
chile peppers (see Note 1)

1 tablespoon **Chef Paul
Prudhomme's Meat Magic**

1 teaspoon ground coriander

•

2¾ cups finely diced onions, in all

¼ cup cider vinegar

1 (4-pound) chicken, all visible fat
removed, cut into 6 pieces

6 cups chicken stock (see page 196)

3 scrubbed carrots, halved

2 unpeeled onions, halved

1 whole garlic bulb, sliced in half
crosswise

1 bunch celery, tough outer stalks
discarded

3 tablespoons unsalted butter

2 cups chopped green bell peppers

3 tablespoons dark brown sugar,
in all

2 ounces unsweetened baking
chocolate, cut into 4 pieces

¼ cup chunky peanut butter

1 (8¼-ounce) bottle green mole
sauce (see Note 2)

20 corn tortillas

1½ cups grated Monterey Jack
cheese

Sour cream, optional

continued

Combine the seasoning mix ingredients in a small bowl.

Combine ¾ *cup* of the diced onions with the vinegar and set aside.

Place the chicken, stock, carrots, halved onions, garlic, and celery in a large heavy pot over high heat, cover, and bring to a boil. Reduce the heat to low and simmer until the chicken is tender, about 40 minutes. Remove from the heat and remove the chicken from the stock. When the chicken is cool enough to handle, remove the skin and bones and discard them. Shred the chicken meat and set it aside.

Strain the cooking stock and skim off the fat. Measure 5 cups and reserve the rest (you can freeze it) for other recipes that call for rich stock.

To make the sauce, melt the butter in a 12-inch skillet over high heat. When the butter sizzles, add the remaining 2 cups chopped onions and the bell peppers and cook for 2 minutes without stirring. Stir in *3 tablespoons* of the seasoning mix and cook, stirring occasionally, for 5 minutes. Add ½ *cup* of the stock and *1 tablespoon* of the brown sugar. Cook, stirring occasionally, until the mixture begins to stick to the bottom of the skillet, about 4 minutes. Add another ½ *cup* stock and scrape up the crust on the skillet bottom. Stir in the chocolate, peanut butter, and mole sauce and cook, stirring occasionally, for 3 minutes. Add the remaining 4 cups stock and the remaining seasoning mix and 2 tablespoons brown sugar. Bring to a boil and cook, stirring occasionally, for 4 minutes. Cook, whisking constantly, until the sauce thickens, turns dark brown, and comes to a bubbling boil. Reduce the heat to low and cook, whisking, for 1 minute. Remove from the heat and let cool.

Preheat the broiler.

Pour 1 cup of the cooled sauce over the shredded chicken and work it in well with your hands.

Drain the vinegar from the reserved diced onions.

Assemble the tostadas in 2 batches. Arrange 10 of the tortillas on a baking sheet and place under the broiler until they are firm, about 1 to 2 minutes. Remove from the broiler and spread 2 tablespoons of the sauce over each of 5 tortillas. Spread ½ cup chicken over the sauce on each tortilla, sprinkle 1 tablespoon of the drained chopped onions over the chicken, and spread another 1 tablespoon sauce over the onions. Place a tortilla on top of each and sprinkle 2 tablespoons of the grated cheese over each tostada. Place under the broiler for 2 minutes, turn the baking sheet around, and broil until browned and bubbly on top, about 2 minutes more. Repeat the process to make 5 more tostadas.

Serve immediately, with sour cream if desired.

NOTE 1: These are the chile peppers we used. Use whatever varieties are available in your area, but use pure ground chile peppers, not commercial chili powder.

NOTE 2: If you can't find bottled mole sauce, you can make your own with one of the following recipes.

Mole Sauce 1

½ cup pumpkin seeds, finely pulverized in a grinder

1 (8-ounce) can salsa verde

Combine the ground pumpkin seeds and salsa verde in a small saucepan over medium-high heat. Cook, stirring often, until thickened and thoroughly blended, about 15 minutes.

Mole Sauce 2

⅓ cup pumpkin seeds
1 tablespoon dried cilantro leaves
2 fresh chile peppers (preferably jalapeños or serranos)

8 tomatillos, chopped
1 small onion, coarsely chopped

Combine all the ingredients in a food processor and process until finely chopped and thoroughly blended. Pour into a saucepan and cook over medium-high heat, stirring often, until thickened, about 15 minutes.

Sticky Chicken

MAKES **6** TO **8** SERVINGS

My mother cooked chickens this way when I was a child. I redid this recipe many years ago, and wherever I go, especially Atlanta, someone always comes up to tell me it's one of their favorites.

4 tablespoons **Chef Paul Prudhomme's Poultry Magic,** in all	Vegetable oil
	3 cups chopped onions
	1 cup chopped celery
1 (5- to 6-pound) stewing chicken, cut up	6½ cups chicken stock (see page 196)
1½ cups all-purpose flour	Hot cooked rice or boiled potatoes

Sprinkle *4 teaspoons* of the Poultry Magic evenly all over the chicken and rub it in.

Combine the flour with *4 teaspoons* Poultry Magic in a paper or plastic bag. Add the seasoned chicken pieces and shake until the chicken is well coated. Reserve the leftover seasoned flour to make the roux.

In a large skillet, heat 1 inch of oil to between 230° and 250° and add the chicken. Use an electric skillet or cooking thermometer and adjust the heat to keep the oil's temperature at a level just hot enough for the chicken to boil instead of fry. This tenderizes the chicken and brings the gelatin from within the bones to the surface. Cook pieces of similar size together to ensure even cooking. Boil with the skin side down for 20 minutes, then on the other side for 15 minutes more. Drain the chicken on paper towels.

Remove the skillet from the heat and let cool for 15 minutes. Pour the oil into a large glass bowl, leaving the sediment in the pan. Pour ½ cup of the cooled oil back into the skillet and place over high heat. Slowly whisk in ¾ cup of the reserved seasoned flour and cook, whisking constantly, until the roux is smooth and medium-brown, about 2 to 3 minutes, being careful not to let it scorch or splash on your skin. Immediately stir in the onions and celery and continue cooking, stirring constantly, until the onions are wilted, about 5 minutes. Remove from the heat.

Bring the stock to a boil in a 4-quart pot and add the roux by spoonfuls, blending well after each addition. Add the chicken pieces and remaining 4 teaspoons of Poultry Magic, reduce the heat to low, and simmer, uncovered, stirring often, for 1 hour. Check the chicken for tenderness and simmer longer if necessary. When tender, serve over the rice or with the boiled potatoes.

SEE COLOR PHOTOGRAPH

Tropical Chicken

This delicious chicken couldn't be easier to prepare, but notice that it is marinated for at least 4 hours, preferably overnight, so you'll want to plan accordingly. The combination of spices and tangy fruit flavors makes me think of faraway places.

SEASONING MIX

1 tablespoon plus 2 teaspoons **Chef Paul Prudhomme's Poultry Magic**

1 teaspoon dried dill weed

½ teaspoon ground ginger

¼ teaspoon ground cardamom

•

MARINADE

2 tablespoons apple juice

2 tablespoons orange juice

1 tablespoon lemon juice

1 tablespoon balsamic vinegar

1 tablespoon seasoning mix

•

1 (3- to 4-pound) chicken, all skin and visible fat removed (don't worry about trying to skin the wings), cut into 8 pieces

2 cups apple juice

1½ cups chopped onions

1 cup chopped green bell peppers

½ cup grated carrots

1 teaspoon minced fresh garlic

1 (8-ounce) can tomato sauce

1 cup peeled (see page 3), diced fresh tomatoes, or 7 ounces canned diced tomatoes

1 cup defatted chicken stock (see page 2)

4 cups cooked long-grain white rice

Combine the seasoning mix ingredients in a small bowl.

Blend the marinade ingredients. Place the chicken in a large bowl, pour the marinade over the chicken, cover, and refrigerate at least 4 hours, but preferably overnight.

Preheat the broiler. Remove the chicken from the marinade and reserve the marinade. Place the chicken in a baking pan and broil until brown on both sides, about 7 minutes in all. Remove the chicken and set aside.

While the chicken is broiling, place the apple juice in a saucepan, bring to a boil, reduce to 1 cup, and set aside.

Preheat a heavy 5-quart pot, preferably nonstick, over high heat to 350°, about 4 minutes.

Add the onions, bell peppers, carrots, and *2 teaspoons* of the seasoning mix; cover and cook for 3 minutes. Add the garlic, mix in well, and scrape the bottom of the pot to clear it of all brown bits. Cover and cook 3 more minutes. Add the reduced apple juice and the remaining seasoning mix, scrape the bottom clear, and cook 4 minutes. Stir in the tomato sauce, diced tomatoes, stock, and reserved marinade. Add the chicken to the pot, bring to a boil, reduce the heat to medium, and cook until the meat is tender, about 20 minutes. Serve over the rice.

Chicken Cacciatore

MAKES **4** SERVINGS

This famous dish, one of the most popular Italian imports, can be prepared ahead and warmed up at serving time, and if there should happen to be any left over, it's just as good the next day. The name means "hunter's style," possibly because the dish always contains mushrooms.

SEASONING MIX
3 tablespoons **Chef Paul Prudhomme's Poultry Magic**
2 teaspoons dried parsley leaves
2 teaspoons dried oregano leaves

•

1 (3- to 3½-pound) chicken, all visible fat removed, cut into 8 pieces
2 (16-ounce) cans whole tomatoes with their liquid
2 tablespoons olive oil
1 cup chopped onions

1 cup chopped green bell peppers
1 cup chopped fresh mushrooms
1 cup dry red wine, in all
1 (6-ounce) can tomato paste
½ teaspoon minced fresh garlic
2 cups chicken stock, in all (see page 196)
1 cup julienne onions (see page 4)
2 cups julienne green bell peppers (see page 4)
¼ cup sliced fresh garlic
3 tablespoons dark brown sugar
2 cups sliced fresh mushrooms

Combine the seasoning mix ingredients in a small bowl.

Sprinkle *1 tablespoon* of the seasoning mix evenly over the chicken and rub it in well.

Pour the tomatoes and their liquid into a bowl and crush them with your hands.

Heat the oil in a heavy 5-quart pot over high heat until very hot, about 4 minutes. Add the chicken pieces, skin side down, and cook, turning once or twice, until just golden brown on all sides, about 8 to 10 minutes. You may have to cook the chicken in batches. Remove the chicken to a bowl and set aside.

Add the chopped onions, bell peppers, and mushrooms to the oil in the pot and scrape up all the browned bits on the bottom. Cook, stirring occasionally, until the vegetables are lightly browned and beginning to stick to the pot, about 5 minutes. Add ½ *cup* of the wine and scrape the pot bottom clean. Cook, stirring occasionally, for 3 to 5 minutes. Stir in the tomato paste and cook, scraping the bottom of the pot from time to time, about 4 minutes. Add *2 tablespoons* of the seasoning mix and cook, stirring, about 1 minute. Stir in the crushed tomatoes and the minced garlic, scrape the bottom of the pot clean, and bring to a bubbling boil. Add the remaining seasoning mix, the remaining ½ cup wine, and *1 cup* of the stock. Stir in the julienne onions and bell peppers and the sliced garlic and cook, stirring occasionally, for 4 minutes.

Return the chicken and any accumulated juices to the pot, stir, and bring to a bubbling boil. Cover the pot, reduce the heat to medium, and simmer for 2 minutes. Stir in the remaining 1 cup stock, cover, and simmer for 7 minutes. Stir in the brown sugar, cover, and simmer for 5 minutes. Add the sliced mushrooms and simmer for 5 minutes. The sauce should be a rich, dark reddish brown. Serve 2 pieces of chicken per person with about 1 cup of sauce over your favorite pasta, and you can freeze any leftover sauce for another pasta dinner.

Basque Chicken and Shrimp in Wine

MAKES **4** TO **8** SERVINGS

This traditional dish from the Basque region of Spain boasts a blend of tantalizingly subtle flavors that we've rounded out with a complement of seasonings. Serve with thick slices of peasant bread and a salad of crisp greens in a light olive oil dressing, and you'll have a perfect Basque meal.

SEASONING MIX
2 tablespoons **Chef Paul Prudhomme's Meat Magic**
1 tablespoon plus 1 teaspoon **Chef Paul Prudhomme's Seafood Magic**

•

1 (2½- to 3-pound) chicken, all visible fat removed, cut into 8 pieces

1 pound peeled shrimp, about 1½ pounds unpeeled
2 tablespoons olive oil
2 cups diced lean ham, about ½ pound
1½ cups chopped onions
¼ cup all-purpose flour
1¼ cups dry white wine, in all
2 cups chicken stock (see page 196)

Combine the seasoning mix ingredients in a small bowl.

Sprinkle *1 tablespoon* of the seasoning mix over the chicken pieces and rub it in well. Sprinkle *1½ teaspoons* of the mix over the shrimp and rub it in well. Set aside.

Heat the oil in a heavy 12-inch skillet over high heat. When the oil is very hot, after about 4 minutes, add the chicken pieces, in batches if necessary, and brown them on all sides, about 8 to 10 minutes. Transfer the chicken to a bowl and set aside.

Add the ham to the oil in the skillet and cook, stirring once or twice, for 2 minutes. Add the onions and *1 tablespoon* of the seasoning mix, and cook until a crust forms on the bottom of the skillet, about 6 to 8 minutes. Stir in the flour and cook until the crust hardens, about 2 to 3 minutes. Add *1 cup* of the wine and scrape the bottom of the skillet fairly clean. Cook, scraping to keep the mixture from sticking, for 2 minutes. Stir in the stock, scrape the skillet bottom, and bring to a boil. Stir in the remaining seasoning mix and bring to a rolling boil.

Preheat the oven to 350°.

Blend in the remaining ¼ cup wine and cook for 2 minutes. Remove from the heat.

Put the chicken and any accumulated juices in an ovenproof casserole or baking pan. Arrange the shrimp over the chicken, and pour the sauce over all. Cover the casserole and bake until the chicken is cooked through, about 30 minutes.

Cheese and Hot Pepper Chicken

MAKES 8 SERVINGS

The sauce for this chicken dish is not only rich and creamy, but also generously seasoned with bell peppers, chile peppers, and spices. Any leftover sauce is wonderful over vegetables!

SEASONING MIX
6 tablespoons **Chef Paul
  Prudhomme's Poultry Magic**
1 teaspoon ground cinnamon
½ teaspoon ground cumin

•

2 (2½- to 3-pound) chickens, all
  visible fat removed, each cut into
  8 pieces
1¼ cups all-purpose flour
Vegetable oil for frying
2⅔ cups chopped green bell
  peppers, in all
2 cups chopped onions
1 cup chopped fresh green Anaheim
  or poblano chiles, in all (see
  Note)

2 bay leaves
2 teaspoons salt
2 teaspoons minced fresh garlic
2 tablespoons finely diced fresh
  jalapeño peppers
4 cups chicken stock, in all
  (see page 196)
1½ cups heavy cream
1 cup dairy sour cream
1½ cups grated Monterey Jack or
  other white nonprocessed cheese
1½ cups grated Cheddar cheese
4 cups cooked long-grain white rice

Remove the chicken from the refrigerator and let it come to room temperature while you prepare the other ingredients.

Combine the seasoning mix ingredients in a small bowl. Combine *1 tablespoon* of the mix with the flour in a plastic or paper bag and set aside.

Sprinkle the remaining seasoning mix evenly over the chicken and rub it in well. Dredge the chicken in the seasoned flour and reserve the leftover flour.

Heat ½ inch of oil in a large skillet (I find this dish tastes significantly better if you *don't* use a nonstick skillet) to 350°, about 4 minutes. Fry the chicken in batches, large pieces and skin side down first, just until lightly browned and crispy, about 2 to 4 minutes per side. Lower the heat if the drippings in the pan start to brown, because you'll use the drippings in the cream sauce—they should remain light in color and taste so they won't dominate the cheese, peppers, and cream. Drain the chicken on paper towels.

Carefully pour the hot oil into a heatproof glass measuring cup, leaving as much sediment as possible in the skillet, and return ½ cup of the hot oil to the skillet. Add *2 cups* of the bell peppers, the onions, and ⅔ *cup* of the chiles. Turn the heat to high and stir well to mix the vegetables with the sediment. Cook until the onions start to brown, stirring occasionally, about 6 to 8 minutes. Add the bay leaves, salt, and garlic. Stir well, then sprinkle 3 tablespoons of the reserved seasoned flour on the vegetable mixture and stir thoroughly again. Stir in the jalapeño peppers and cook, stirring occasionally, for 2 minutes. Lower the heat if the vegetables stick excessively. Stir in *1 cup* of the stock and scrape the pan bottom well. Stir in *2 cups* more stock and stir again. Remove from the heat.

Place the chicken in a 5½-quart pot or Dutch oven. Add the vegetable mixture and the remaining 1 cup stock and stir well. Bring to a boil over high heat, reduce the heat to low, and simmer, stirring occasionally and being careful not to let the mixture scorch, for 25 minutes. Add the remaining ⅔ cup bell peppers, ⅓ cup chiles, the cream, and the sour cream. Bring to a boil over medium heat, stirring fairly constantly. Stir in the cheeses and

continued

cook, stirring constantly, just until the cheese melts. Serve immediately over the rice.

NOTE: If you cannot find fresh Anaheim or poblano chile peppers, you can use canned chile pepper strips, either hot or mild, according to your taste.

☆

Chicken Paprika

MAKES **4** SERVINGS

This is our version of the traditional Hungarian favorite, a dish that people from all over the world enjoy. It's another recipe that is easy to prepare but makes a great presentation and has an exciting flavor. It's important to taste your paprika to be sure it's sweet, because if it's bitter it will ruin the dish. Paprika that is old and often dark is likely to be bitter, and this spice varies widely from brand to brand.

3 tablespoons *Chef Paul Prudhomme's Poultry Magic,* in all

1 (3- to 4-pound) chicken, all visible fat removed, cut into 8 pieces

2 tablespoons olive oil

2 cups chopped onions, in all

1 teaspoon minced fresh garlic

¼ cup sweet paprika

½ teaspoon dried dill weed

1 teaspoon dried basil leaves

1 (6-ounce) can tomato paste

3½ cups chicken stock (see page 196)

1 (8-ounce) container sour cream

4 cups cooked wide egg noodles

Sprinkle *2 tablespoons* of the Poultry Magic over the chicken and rub it in well; set aside.

Heat the oil in a heavy 5½-quart pot over high heat for 4 minutes. Brown the chicken pieces for 5 minutes on each side (you may have to do this in batches) and remove to a bowl. Add *1 cup* of the onions to the pot, scrape up the brown crust on the bottom, and cook for 2 minutes. Add the garlic, paprika, remaining 1 tablespoon Poultry Magic, dill, basil, and remaining onions. Cook, scraping the bottom of the pot occasionally, until the onions are golden brown and a crust forms, about 4 minutes. Stir in the tomato paste, scrape the pot bottom, and cook for 2 minutes. Add the stock, scrape up the crust on the bottom of the pot, and bring to a boil. Return the chicken and any juices that have accumulated to the pot, and bring to a boil. Reduce the heat to medium–low, cover, and simmer until the chicken is done, about 25 minutes.

Remove the pot from the heat. Stir several tablespoons of the sauce into the sour cream, then gently stir the sour cream mixture back into the sauce. Place the pot back over low heat and cook, stirring constantly, just until all the sour cream is incorporated and the sauce is heated through. Serve over the noodles.

Down-Home Roast Chicken

MAKES **4** SERVINGS

This chicken is great served with its gravy over rice or mashed potatoes. If you've never roasted poultry in a very slow oven for a very long time, you're going to be pleasantly surprised at how tender and juicy it is. And you'll be pleased at how little prep time it requires. People often ask what's the secret to my great roast chicken, and now you know!

4 tablespoons unsalted butter
2 cups chopped onions
1 cup chopped bell peppers
4 tablespoons plus 1 teaspoon **Chef Paul Prudhomme's Poultry Magic,** in all

1 (3½- to 4-pound) roasting chicken
¼ cup all-purpose flour
2 teaspoons **Chef Paul Prudhomme's Meat Magic**
2 cups chicken stock (see page 196)

Preheat an 8-inch skillet over high heat for 2 minutes. Add the butter, onions, bell peppers, and *3 tablespoons* of the Poultry Magic. Cook, scraping the bottom of the skillet occasionally, until the vegetables are golden brown, about 10 minutes. Remove from the heat and let cool.

Preheat the oven to 250°. Remove the giblets from the chicken and clean out the cavity. Stuff the cavity with the cooled vegetables, fold the skin flaps over to keep the vegetables in, and secure with poultry pins or toothpicks. Sprinkle the remaining Poultry Magic evenly over the chicken and rub it in well.

Place the chicken, breast side up, in a large roasting pan without a rack, and secure the drumsticks and wings close to the body with poultry pins or twine. Roast, uncovered, until tender, about 2½ hours. Remove the chicken from the oven and set it aside until cool enough to handle. Be careful at this stage—the chicken may be very hot inside, even if cool to the touch on the surface. With a long-handled spoon, remove the vegetables and place them in the pan, along with any juices from the cavity. Remove the chicken from the pan and set it aside.

Place the pan over high heat. Add the flour and Meat Magic to the vegetables, blending until they are completely absorbed. Whisk in the stock and bring to a boil, whisking until thoroughly blended, about 1 to 2 minutes. Makes 3 cups of gravy.

☆

Turkey Rex

MAKES **8** CUPS, ENOUGH FOR **4** GENEROUS SERVINGS

This traditional-tasting dish can be made with fresh turkey or chicken, but is also a great way to use leftover holiday bird. If you use cooked turkey, then season and add it toward the end of the cooking time, so it doesn't overcook.

continued

1 pound turkey (or chicken) breast, cut into ¾-inch cubes

1 tablespoon plus 1 teaspoon **Chef Paul Prudhomme's Poultry Magic**, in all

1 cup chopped onions

¾ cup chopped red bell peppers

¾ cup chopped yellow bell peppers

¾ cup chopped green bell peppers

3 cups sliced fresh mushrooms

2½ cups defatted chicken stock, in all (see page 2)

10 tablespoons nonfat dry milk

3 tablespoons all-purpose flour

½ cup nonfat cream cheese

6 cups cooked long-grain white rice

Preheat a heavy 5-quart pot, preferably nonstick, over high heat to 350°, about 4 minutes.

Sprinkle all surfaces of the turkey cubes evenly with *2 teaspoons* of the Poultry Magic and rub it in well. Spread the seasoned turkey cubes evenly over the bottom of the pot and cook, turning as necessary, until they are browned on all sides, about 3 to 5 minutes. Add the onions, peppers, mushrooms, and remaining Poultry Magic. Cook, stirring occasionally, for 4 minutes.

While the mixture is cooking, place *1 cup* of the stock in a blender, add the dry milk and flour, and process until smooth and creamy. Transfer this mixture to the pot and add the remaining stock. Cook just until it comes to a gentle boil, about 3 minutes. Lower the heat and simmer 4 to 6 minutes. Turn off the heat. Remove 1 cup of the liquid from the pot, place it in the blender, add the cream cheese, and blend. Stir this mixture back into the pot and serve immediately over the rice.

Hot and Sweet Turkey

★★★★★★

This recipe is always a favorite when we prepare it on the road, and people can't believe it's a no-added-fat dish. Because of the fresh ginger and tamari sauce, the flavor has just a hint of the exotic, but it's easy to make, so you can enjoy it often.

SEASONING MIX

2 tablespoons **Chef Paul Prudhomme's Poultry Magic**

½ teaspoon ground ginger

¼ teaspoon ground nutmeg

¼ teaspoon ground coriander

•

1 pound turkey (or chicken) breast meat, cut into julienne strips (see page 4)

3 tablespoons cornstarch

2½ cups defatted chicken stock, in all (see page 2)

¼ cup thinly sliced fresh ginger

1 small onion, peeled and cut into julienne strips (see page 4)

¾ cup carrots, scrubbed and sliced diagonally ¼ inch thick

¾ cup julienne red bell peppers (see page 4)

¾ cup julienne yellow bell peppers (see page 4)

¾ cup julienne green bell peppers (see page 4)

2 teaspoons thinly sliced fresh garlic

¼ cup tamari (see Note)

¼ cup balsamic vinegar

1 (8-ounce) can tomato sauce

6 (1-gram) packets artificial sweetener, optional

4 cups cooked long-grain white rice

continued

Combine the seasoning mix ingredients in a small bowl.

Sprinkle all surfaces of the turkey evenly with *2 teaspoons* of the seasoning mix and rub it in well. Dissolve the cornstarch in *¼ cup* of the stock and set aside.

Preheat a heavy 12-inch skillet, preferably nonstick, over high heat to 350°, about 5 minutes. Add the turkey, stir, and cook until it starts to brown, about 2 minutes. Add the fresh ginger and onion, stir, and cook for 2 minutes. Add the remaining vegetables and seasoning mix, stir, and cook for 3 minutes. Stir in the tamari and vinegar and cook, stirring occasionally, until much of the liquid evaporates and the sauce becomes thick and syrupy. Stir in the tomato sauce and remaining stock, bring to a boil, and cook for 2 minutes. Add the cornstarch mixture, cook for 2 minutes, and remove from the heat; if desired, stir in the artificial sweetener. Serve over the rice.

NOTE: Tamari is a very flavorful kind of soy sauce, available in specialty markets and the international or ethnic food sections of many supermarkets. If it is unavailable where you shop, use the best soy sauce you can find.

Off the Hoof

Navajo Tacos

★☆★☆★☆★

Our version of this traditional recipe uses more varieties of chile peppers—green and dried—than most, but I think they give the dish a magnificent flavor.

SALSA

2 chopped fresh serrano chile peppers (see Note)

3 chopped large fresh Anaheim peppers (see Note)

2 chopped fresh cayenne peppers (see Note)

3 chopped fresh jalapeño peppers (see Note)

¾ cup chopped green bell peppers

1½ cups chopped onions

1 cup packed chopped fresh cilantro

4 large fresh tomatoes, coarsely chopped

2 tablespoons vinegar

Juice of 1 lemon

2 tablespoons dark brown sugar

2 tablespoons **Chef Paul Prudhomme's Magic Pepper Sauce**

●

SEASONING MIX

2 tablespoons plus 1 teaspoon **Chef Paul Prudhomme's Meat Magic**

2 teaspoons ground dried guajillo chile peppers (see Note)

1¾ teaspoons ground dried arbol chile peppers (see Note)

1½ teaspoons dried oregano leaves

●

continued

FILLING

1 small lamb roast, approximately
    1½ pounds if boneless, 2 pounds
    if bone-in, or 1½ pounds lamb
    stew meat
Seasoning mix
2 cups chopped onions
4 tablespoons unsalted butter
1 (4-ounce) can chopped green
    chiles
2 sliced large garlic cloves
1 cup chopped green bell peppers
½ cup chopped fresh Anaheim (or
    any mild) chile peppers
¼ cup all-purpose flour
2¾ cups chicken stock
    (see page 196)

INDIAN FRY-BREAD

5 cups all-purpose flour, in all
½ cup powdered nondairy creamer
1 tablespoon plus 1 teaspoon
    baking powder
½ cup dry milk
1 teaspoon salt
2 cups water
1 tablespoon **Chef Paul
    Prudhomme's Magic Pepper
    Sauce**
3 to 4 cups vegetable oil

•

TO MAKE THE SALSA: Combine the peppers, onions, and cilantro in a large bowl. Stir in the tomatoes, vinegar, lemon juice, sugar, and Magic Pepper Sauce. Blend thoroughly and set aside.

TO MAKE THE SEASONING MIX: Combine all the ingredients in a small bowl.

TO MAKE THE FILLING: Cut all the visible fat from the lamb, chop the fat into small pieces, and set it aside.

Cut the lamb into 1-inch cubes, sprinkle with *1 tablespoon plus 1 teaspoon* of the seasoning mix, and rub in well. Set aside.

Render the reserved lamb fat in a 10-inch skillet over high heat until fairly dark and smoky, about 4 to 6 minutes. Add the onions and *2 teaspoons* of the seasoning mix. Stir once and cook until the onions start sticking to the bottom of the pan, about 4 minutes. Stir in the butter. As soon as the butter melts, add the lamb. Scrape up the crust on the bottom of the skillet and cook, scraping the pan bottom occasionally, for 10 minutes. Stir in the chiles and garlic and cook for 2 minutes. Stir in the bell peppers, Anaheim peppers, and the remaining seasoning mix and cook for 2 minutes. Stir in the flour and cook, scraping the bottom of the pan occasionally, for 3 minutes. Stir in *2 cups* of the stock, scrape up the crust on the bottom of the skillet, and bring to a bubbling boil. Reduce the heat to medium and simmer, uncovered, for 5 minutes. The mixture should be thick and dark. Stir in the remaining stock and cook until the mixture reduces slightly, about 11 minutes. Remove from the heat and keep warm. Makes about 5 cups.

TO MAKE THE FRY-BREAD: Sift *4 cups* of the flour, the nondairy creamer, baking powder, dry milk, and salt together. Add the water and Magic Pepper Sauce and mix well until a soft dough forms. Sift the remaining 1 cup flour over a work surface and flour your hands thoroughly. Pull off a large handful of the dough and pat it out with floured hands into a thin, flat, round cake. Keep flouring the work surface and your hands as you form cakes from the remaining dough. You should have 10 cakes.

Heat *2 cups* of the oil in an 8-inch skillet over high heat until very hot, about 3½ minutes. Fry the cakes one at a time, turning two or three times, until golden brown, about 30 to 45 seconds. Drain thoroughly on paper towels. Add oil as necessary and allow it to get hot before frying additional cakes.

Cover each round of fry-bread with ½ cup of the lamb mixture, top with salsa, and serve immediately.

NOTE: If you can't find the fresh peppers we used, substitute peppers of similar heat intensities. The cayennes are the hottest of those we used, the serranos almost as hot, the jalapeños a bit milder, and the Anaheims very mild. The manager of the produce department where you shop should be able to help you with selection. If you can't find the dried chile peppers we used, use what is available in your area, but don't use commercial chili powder.

La Jolla Tamale Pie

This hearty, stick-to-the-ribs dish is seasoned with a variety of chile peppers, but if you can't find all the varieties we specify, use whatever are available where you shop. Our recipe for tamale pie uses cornmeal as part of the filling, not just on top.

SEASONING MIX

2 tablespoons plus 1 teaspoon **Chef Paul Prudhomme's Meat Magic**

2 tablespoons plus 1 teaspoon **Chef Paul Prudhomme's Seafood Magic**

1 tablespoon plus ¼ teaspoon ground dried New Mexico chile peppers (see page 2)

2½ teaspoons ground dried arbol chile peppers (see page 2)

2½ teaspoons ground dried pasilla chile peppers (see page 2)

1½ pounds ground lean pork

¼ cup olive oil, in all

3 cups chopped onions, in all

2 cups chopped green bell peppers, in all

2¼ cups yellow cornmeal, in all

4 tablespoons unsalted butter

2 teaspoons minced fresh garlic

5½ cups beef stock, in all (see page 198)

2 tablespoons dark brown sugar

1 cup sliced pitted large black olives

Vegetable oil cooking spray

Combine the seasoning mix ingredients in a small bowl.

Sprinkle *2 tablespoons* of the seasoning mix evenly over the ground pork and blend it in well with your hands. Set aside the remaining seasoning mix.

Heat *3 tablespoons* of the olive oil in a 12-inch skillet over high heat. When the oil sizzles, add *2 cups* of the onions, *1 cup* of the bell peppers, and *1 tablespoon* of the seasoning mix. Cook, stirring occasionally, until the onions are golden, about 4 to 6 minutes. Stir in *1 cup* of the cornmeal and the butter and cook, stirring occasionally, until the cornmeal is dark and sticking to the bottom of the skillet, about 4 to 5 minutes. Add the garlic and *1 tablespoon* of the seasoning mix, scrape the skillet bottom, and cook for 2 minutes. Stir in *3½ cups* of the stock and the brown sugar and scrape the bottom of the skillet clean. Stir the mixture constantly, and as soon as it starts to bubble, stir in *¾ cup* of the cornmeal. Reduce the heat to medium and simmer, stirring occasionally, for 14 minutes. Remove from the heat.

Heat the remaining 1 tablespoon olive oil in a 10-inch skillet over high heat. When the oil is hot, about 3 minutes, add the remaining onions, bell peppers, and seasoning mix. Cook, stirring occasionally, until the vegetables are lightly browned, about 6 minutes. Move the vegetables to one side of the skillet and add the seasoned pork to the cleared space. Break up any lumps of meat with a spoon and cook until lightly browned, about 2 minutes. Stir the pork into the vegetables and cook, stirring occasionally, until the pork and vegetables are well browned, about 5 minutes. Stir in the remaining ½ cup cornmeal. Cook until a crust forms on the bottom of the skillet, scrape it up, and cook until another crust forms, about 4 minutes in all. Stir in *1 cup* of the stock and the olives, scrape the bottom of the skillet clean, and cook for 4 minutes. Add the remaining 1 cup stock, scrape the skillet bottom, and remove from the heat.

Preheat the oven to 350°.

Coat a 10-inch cake pan or springform pan with cooking spray and spread one-third the cornmeal mixture over the bottom of the pan. Spread half the pork filling over the cornmeal. Spread half the remaining cornmeal mixture evenly over the pork, spread another layer of pork filling, and finish with a layer of the cornmeal mixture on top. Bake until brown, about 30 minutes. Serve warm.

Roasted Pork with Gingersnap Gravy

MAKES **6** SERVINGS

When we tested this recipe for this book, several of our tasters said it was the very best roast they had ever eaten! The ginger flavor, present but subtle, adds an unusual but very complementary touch to the pork. Not only is this roast delicious, but it makes an impressive presentation, so you'll be proud to serve it on special occasions.

3 tablespoons unsalted butter

1 tablespoon pork lard, chicken fat, or vegetable oil

½ cup finely diced onions

½ cup finely diced green bell peppers

½ cup finely diced celery

1 tablespoon minced fresh garlic

2 tablespoons **Chef Paul Prudhomme's Vegetable Magic**

½ teaspoon dry mustard

1 (4-pound) boneless pork loin roast

Melt the butter and lard (or fat or oil) in a large skillet over high heat. Add the vegetables and seasonings and cook, stirring occasionally, for 4 minutes. Remove from the heat and let cool.

Preheat the oven to 275°.

Place the roast in a baking pan, fat side up. Make several large slits in the top of the meat with a knife, being careful not to cut through to the bottom. Stuff the pockets with some of the cooled vegetable mixture, then spread the remaining mixture over the top and sides of the meat. Roast, uncovered, for 3 hours, then raise the temperature to 425° and roast until the meat is dark brown on top and white in the center, about 10 to 15 minutes. Serve with Gingersnap Gravy.

Gingersnap Gravy

MAKES ABOUT 2½ CUPS

8 gingersnap cookies

2 tablespoons pork lard, chicken fat, or vegetable oil

2 tablespoons unsalted butter

¾ cup finely diced onions

½ cup finely diced celery

½ teaspoon minced garlic

1 tablespoon **Chef Paul Prudhomme's Meat Magic**

6 cups pork or chicken stock (see page 198 or 196)

1 cup pan drippings from roasted pork (add stock if needed to make 1 cup)

1 tablespoon light brown sugar, or to taste

1 teaspoon ground ginger, or to taste

Crush the cookies with a rolling pin on a hard surface to make fine crumbs and set aside.

Melt the lard (or fat or oil) and butter in a large skillet over medium heat. When almost melted, add the onions, celery, and garlic and cook, stirring occasionally, for 5 minutes. Stir in the Meat Magic and cook, stirring occasionally, for 5 minutes more. Add the stock and pan drippings, bring to a boil over high heat, and boil rapidly until the liquid is reduced to about 1 quart, about 25 minutes. Stir in the cookie crumbs and cook, stirring frequently, for 10 minutes. Taste the gravy; if the ginger flavor is not pronounced enough, add the brown sugar and ground ginger and stir to combine. Strain the gravy before serving.

SEE COLOR PHOTOGRAPH

Pork Curry

MAKES **6** SERVINGS

★ ☆ ★ ☆ ★ ☆

I love Indian food, especially curry, and don't care if it's made with chicken, beef, or pork, as this one is. If you want less heat, use only half the jalapeño peppers. Many people like to serve condiments with curry—flaked coconut, additional nuts, chutney, toasted seeds—and all are great. When we serve this at my New Orleans restaurant, we always get rave reviews from locals as well as tourists.

1 pound boneless pork Boston butt or boneless pork shoulder, cut into bite-size chunks

1 tablespoon plus 2½ teaspoons **Chef Paul Prudhomme's Pork and Veal Magic***, in all*

1 tablespoon plus 2½ teaspoons curry powder

1 teaspoon ground turmeric

1 teaspoon dried thyme leaves

1 teaspoon ground cumin

½ teaspoon ground cinnamon

3 tablespoons pork lard, chicken fat, or butter

¼ pound (1 stick) unsalted butter

2 cups chopped onions, in all

6 tablespoons minced fresh jalapeño peppers, in all

1½ cups chopped unpeeled apples

½ cup dry-roasted pecan halves or pieces

6 tablespoons raisins

1 large overripe banana, mashed, in all

2 cups pork or chicken stock, in all (see page 198 or 196)

¾ cup canned cream of coconut

4½ cups hot cooked white rice

Sprinkle the pork evenly with *2½ teaspoons* of the Pork and Veal Magic and rub it in well. Set aside.

Combine the curry powder, turmeric, thyme, cumin, cinnamon, and *remaining 1 tablespoon* Pork and Veal Magic in a small bowl and set aside.

Melt the lard (or chicken fat) and the 1 stick of butter (or melt 1 stick plus 3 tablespoons of butter) in a 4-quart pot over high heat. Add *1½ cups* of the onions and the seasoning mixture and cook, stirring frequently, for 2 minutes. Reduce the heat to low. Stir in *3 tablespoons* of the jalapeño peppers and cook for 20 minutes, stirring occasionally and more often toward the end of the 20 minutes, scraping the pot bottom well each time. Add the apples, pecans, raisins, and *half* of the banana, stirring well. Continue cooking for 15 minutes, stirring and scraping the pan bottom frequently. At this stage you will see a buildup of browned matter on the pan bottom—easy to scrape off with a spoon—which is what helps give so much flavor to this dish.

Add *½ cup* of the stock, stir well, and cook and stir for 10 minutes. Add *½ cup* more stock and continue cooking for 15 minutes, stirring and scraping the pan bottom frequently. Stir in the cream of coconut, *½ cup* more stock, and the remaining ½ cup onions, and cook and stir for 20 minutes. Add the pork, the remaining ½ cup stock, and the remaining 3 tablespoons jalapeño peppers, and cook and stir for 10 minutes. Add the remaining half banana, and cook and stir for 10 minutes more. Remove from the heat and serve immediately.

To serve, spoon ¾ cup rice around the edges of each serving plate and mound about ¾ cup curry in the center.

SEE COLOR PHOTOGRAPH

Pork Roast with Dill Sauce

I hadn't tasted this recipe in a while, even though it is from one of my cookbooks. When I am working in the test kitchen, I usually taste only very small portions. I have to admit, however, that even though there were six other dishes presented for approval, when the pork roast was served, I couldn't resist spending a great deal of time with this old friend—until the plate was clean.

SEASONING MIX

2 tablespoons **Chef Paul Prudhomme's Pork and Veal Magic**

2 teaspoons ground dried Anaheim chile peppers (see page 2)

2 teaspoons ground dried ancho chile peppers (see page 2)

1 teaspoon dried thyme leaves

½ teaspoon dried dill weed

•

4 tablespoons unsalted butter, in all

1 cup chopped onions

1 cup chopped celery

4 teaspoons grated fresh ginger, in all

1 (5½-pound) boneless pork loin, from the sirloin end

3 branches fresh dill, in all

¼ cup all-purpose flour

½ teaspoon minced fresh garlic

¼ cup minced fresh dill

3 cups beef stock, in all (see page 198)

1½ cups heavy cream, in all

Combine the seasoning mix ingredients in a small bowl.

Melt *2 tablespoons* of the butter in an 8-inch skillet over high heat. When it sizzles, add the onions, celery, *2 teaspoons* of the seasoning mix, and *1 teaspoon* of the ginger. Cook, stirring once or twice, until the vegetables are browned, about 6 to 7 minutes. Remove from the heat and let cool.

Preheat the oven to 350°.

With a small, sharp knife, make slits about 1 inch apart in the top of the roast, taking care not to cut all the way through. Stuff the holes with sprigs of fresh dill pulled from 2 of the branches (reserve 1 large sprig for garnish). Sprinkle *1 tablespoon plus 1 teaspoon* of the seasoning mix evenly over the meat and rub it in well. Spread the vegetable mixture over the top and sides of the roast. Place the meat in a roasting pan and roast until it is fork tender and juicy, about 2¼ hours.

Pour off the drippings from the pan and cover the roast to keep it warm. Skim off ⅓ cup of fat from the drippings and combine it with the remaining 2 tablespoons butter in a 10-inch skillet over high heat. When the butter melts, whisk in the flour. Add the garlic and *2 teaspoons* of the ginger and cook, whisking constantly, for 2 minutes. Add the minced fresh dill and *1½ cups* of the stock and cook, whisking, for 2 minutes. Add *1 cup* of the cream and cook, whisking, for 5 minutes. Add the remaining seasoning mix and cook, whisking, for 2 minutes. Add the remaining cream, ginger, and stock, and cook for 5 minutes, whisking constantly. Remove from the heat.

To serve, slice the roast, drizzle the sauce over it, and garnish with the reserved sprig of fresh dill.

Panéed Veal and Fettucini

MAKES **6** SERVINGS

★ ☆ ★ ☆ ★ ☆

Pané is just a south Louisiana term for quick pan frying. We use the method for thin pieces of many kinds of meat because it preserves the flavor of the meat while still cooking it thoroughly. It works particularly well with a mild-tasting meat like veal, which we've combined with seasonings and tender pasta.

4 quarts hot water

2 tablespoons vegetable oil

1 tablespoon salt

¾ pound fresh fettucini, or ½ pound dry

½ pound (2 sticks) unsalted butter

2½ cups heavy cream

2 tablespoons **Chef Paul Prudhomme's Pork and Veal Magic**, or 2 tablespoons **Chef Paul Prudhomme's Vegetable Magic**, or 1 tablespoon plus 2 teaspoons **Chef Paul Prudhomme's Meat Magic**, in all

¾ cup plus 4 teaspoons finely grated Parmesan cheese (preferably imported), in all

1¾ cups very fine dry bread crumbs

1½ tablespoons minced fresh parsley

1½ tablespoons olive oil

3 eggs

6 (3½- to 4-ounce) slices of baby white veal, pounded thin

Vegetable oil for pan frying

Place the water, oil, and salt in a large pot over high heat, cover, and bring to a rolling boil. Add small amounts of fettucini at a time, breaking up the oil patches as you drop it in. Return to a boil and cook to *al dente* stage (about 3 minutes if using fresh pasta, 7 minutes if dry), but do not overcook. During this cooking time, use a wooden or spaghetti spoon to lift the fettucini out of the water by spoonfuls and shake strands back into the boiling water, a procedure that seems to enhance the pasta's texture. Immediately drain the fettucini in a colander and stop the cooking by running cold water over the strands. (If you use dry pasta, first rinse with hot water to wash off excess starch.) After the pasta has cooled thoroughly, about 2 to 3 minutes, pour about 1 tablespoon of vegetable oil in your hands and gently rub the fettucini until it's well coated with oil. Set aside still in the colander.

Melt the butter in a large skillet over medium-low heat. Add the cream and *1 teaspoon* of the Pork and Veal Magic (or other Magic Seasoning Blend) and raise the heat to medium-high. Whisk the mixture constantly as it comes to a boil, then reduce the heat and simmer, still whisking constantly, until the sauce has reduced some and thickened enough to coat a spoon well, about 7 to 8 minutes. Remove from the heat and gradually add ¾ *cup* of the Parmesan, whisking until the cheese melts, then set aside.

Combine the bread crumbs, parsley, olive oil, and remaining Pork and Veal Magic (or other Magic Seasoning Blend) in a shallow baking pan. Beat the eggs in a separate shallow pan, then beat the remaining 4 teaspoons Parmesan into the eggs. Soak the veal in the egg mixture for at least 5 minutes, being sure to coat it thoroughly.

Meanwhile, heat ¼ inch oil to about 400° in a large skillet. Just before frying, dredge the veal in the seasoned bread crumbs, coating well and pressing the crumbs in with your hands. Shake off any excess. Fry the veal in the hot oil until golden brown, about 1 minute per side. Do not crowd. If any of the crumbs in the bottom start to burn, change the oil immediately. Remove the veal to a large platter and set aside.

Reheat the cheese sauce over medium-high heat, whisking frequently. If the butter starts to separate, whisk in 1 tablespoon of cream or water. Add the fettucini and toss until thoroughly coated and heated through, about 1 minute. Remove from the heat and serve immediately. To serve, place a piece of veal on each heated serving plate. Roll each portion of fettucini onto a large fork and slide onto the plate. Top with additional cheese sauce from the skillet.

Chef Paul's Meat Loaf

MAKES 6 SERVINGS

One of my most requested recipes! There is nothing like a hearty slab of meat loaf and a mound of creamy mashed potatoes to go with it. I think we all have fond memories of our first meat loaf, which usually remains the one that we prefer for the rest of our lives. Try this recipe just one time. If you like it, you have my permission to tell all your friends that this is *your* family recipe.

SEASONING MIX

1 tablespoon plus 2 teaspoons **Chef Paul Prudhomme's Meat Magic**

½ teaspoon ground nutmeg

2 bay leaves

•

4 tablespoons unsalted butter

¾ cup finely chopped onions

½ cup finely chopped celery

½ cup finely chopped green bell peppers

¼ cup finely chopped green onions

2 teaspoons minced fresh garlic

1 tablespoon **Chef Paul Prudhomme's Magic Pepper Sauce**

1 tablespoon Worcestershire sauce

½ cup evaporated milk

½ cup catsup

1½ pounds ground beef

½ pound ground pork

2 eggs, lightly beaten

1 cup very fine dry bread crumbs

Combine the seasoning mix ingredients and set aside.

Melt the butter in a 1-quart saucepan over medium heat. Add the onions, celery, bell peppers, green onions, garlic, Magic Pepper Sauce, Worcestershire sauce, and seasoning mix. Sauté, stirring occasionally and scraping the bottom of the pan, until the mixture starts sticking excessively, about 6 minutes. Stir in the milk and catsup. Continue cooking for about 2 minutes, stirring occasionally. Remove from the heat and allow to cool at room temperature.

Preheat the oven to 350°.

Place the ground meat in an ungreased 13×9-inch baking pan. Add the eggs, the cooked vegetable mixture (remove the bay leaves), and the bread crumbs. Mix by hand until thoroughly combined. Shape the mixture into a loaf that is about 12×6×1½ inches (it will not touch the sides of the pan) and bake, uncovered, for 25 minutes. Raise the heat to 400° and continue baking until done, about 35 minutes longer.

Really Rich Beef and Mushrooms

MAKES **4** SERVINGS

This recipe produces some of the tenderest beef you've ever eaten, and some of the tastiest too. The sauce is so rich—downright sinful—that you would never guess that this is a low-fat dish. So pull yourself up to the table and say, "The devil made me do it!"

SOUR CREAM MIXTURE

12 ounces low-fat cottage cheese

2 ounces nonfat cream cheese

3 tablespoons vinegar

•

SEASONING MIX

1 tablespoon plus 2 teaspoons **Chef Paul Prudhomme's Meat Magic**

1 teaspoon crushed or coarsely ground black pepper

•

1 pound top round steak, all visible fat removed, scalloped (see page 3)

2 cups chopped onions

4 cups defatted beef stock, in all (see page 2)

6 tablespoons all-purpose flour, sifted

8 cups sliced fresh mushrooms

6 cups cooked wide noodles

DAY 1 • Combine the sour cream mixture ingredients in a blender or food processor and purée until smooth and creamy. If the mixture is very thick, push it down toward the blades a few times. Cover and refrigerate overnight.

DAY 2 • Combine the seasoning mix ingredients in a small bowl.

Sprinkle all surfaces of the meat evenly with *2 teaspoons* of the seasoning mix, rub it in well, and set aside.

Preheat a heavy 5-quart pot, preferably nonstick, over high heat to 350°, about 4 minutes. Add the onions and cook just until they start to brown, about 2 to 3 minutes. Move the onions to one side of the pot and add the seasoned meat to the other side, along with the remaining seasoning mix. Cook, stirring the meat once or twice, for 5 minutes. Add *½ cup* of the stock, mix the meat and onions together, and scrape the bottom of the pot to clear it of all brown bits. Cook until most of the liquid evaporates and the mixture starts to stick, about 5 minutes. Add *½ cup* stock and scrape the bottom of the pot again. Stir in the sifted flour and mix until it is completely absorbed (none of the white of the flour is visible), a paste forms, and the beef is moist and sticky. Add the mushrooms, stir, and cook, scraping the bottom of the pot occasionally to prevent sticking, for 5 minutes. Add the remaining stock, stir to clear the bottom and sides of the pot, and cook for 10 minutes. Add the sour cream mixture and whisk until it is completely blended into the sauce. Serve over the wide noodles.

Beef Fajitas

I really like the flavors in Mexican food and especially the taste of this dish. It goes great with all the traditional accompaniments listed. We've called for boneless sirloin strip steaks, but you can use skirt steak or London broil— just be sure the cut is tender enough to broil. Skirt steak is usually about ¼ inch thick, which is perfect; London broil is about ½ inch thick, so you'll need to slice it in half before cutting it into strips.

SEASONING MIX

2 tablespoons **Chef Paul Prudhomme's Meat Magic**

2 teaspoons ground dried guajillo chile peppers (see page 2)

2 teaspoons ground dried ancho chile peppers (see page 2)

•

4 tablespoons (½ stick) unsalted butter, in all

2 cups julienne onions (see page 4)

1 cup julienne red, green, or yellow bell peppers (see page 4)

2 (10-ounce) boneless beef sirloin strip steaks, trimmed and cut into julienne strips (see page 4)

½ cup freshly squeezed lime juice

Warm flour tortillas

Sour cream

Guacamole

Tomato salsa

Shredded lettuce

Combine the seasoning mix ingredients in a small bowl.

Melt *2 tablespoons* of the butter in a heavy 12-inch skillet over high heat. Add the onions and cook, shaking the skillet or stirring occasionally, until they are clear and turning brown on the edges, about 3 minutes. Stir in the bell peppers and cook, continuing to stir or shake the pan, until the onions are soft but the bell peppers are still crunchy, about 3 minutes more. Reduce the heat if necessary to avoid burning the vegetables. Transfer the vegetables to a plate to stop the cooking process. Set the skillet aside without wiping it, to use later for sautéing the meat.

Heat several sizzle platters or a large cast-iron skillet in a 400° oven.

Meanwhile, place the meat strips in a large bowl and sprinkle them with *2 teaspoons* of the seasoning mix, tossing to coat well. Pour the lime juice over the meat and toss again. Let marinate at least 10 minutes, tossing occasionally. (After 15 minutes the meat strips will break apart when pulled.)

Heat the unwiped skillet over high heat for 40 to 45 seconds and add the remaining butter (it will sizzle). Pick up the meat with your fingers, let it drain slightly, and add it to the skillet, reserving the marinade. Cook the meat about 45 seconds, turning frequently to coat with butter. Add the reserved vegetables to the meat and cook for 15 seconds, tossing constantly to combine. Add the reserved marinade, then sprinkle the remaining seasoning mix over all, and cook for 1 minute, still tossing or stirring. Remove from the heat and pour onto the heated sizzle platters or cast-iron skillet. Serve while still sizzling.

Let everyone prepare his or her own fajitas using the traditional condiments. The classic method is to lay some meat and cooked vegetables down the center of a tortilla, spoon on the desired condiments, and then fold one end up, fold one side in, and roll up the remaining side to prevent the goodies from squirting out the end of the tortilla.

Flank and Greens

☆☆☆☆☆☆

This attractive dish is particularly nutritious. Because you don't discard the liquid in which the greens are cooked, it's high in vitamins, and it's low in fat as well. And cooking the greens with the meat gives both an indescribably rich, delicious flavor.

SEASONING MIX
2 tablespoons **Chef Paul Prudhomme's Meat Magic**
1 teaspoon ground ginger
¾ teaspoon ground cumin

●

1½ pounds flank steak, all visible fat removed, scalloped (see page 3)

2 cups chopped onions
12 cups washed and chopped mixed greens, in all (see Note)
6 cups defatted beef stock, in all (see page 2)
5 tablespoons all-purpose flour, browned (see page 3)
6 cups cooked long-grain white rice

Combine the seasoning mix ingredients in a small bowl.

Sprinkle all surfaces of the scalloped steak evenly with *2 teaspoons* of the seasoning mix and rub it in well.

Preheat a heavy 5-quart pot, preferably nonstick, over high heat to 350°, about 4 minutes. Add the seasoned meat and brown it on all sides, about 2 to 3 minutes. Add the onions, the remaining seasoning mix, and ½ *cup* of each type of greens. Cover and cook, scraping the bottom of the pot to clear all the browned bits, for 8 minutes. Add *1 cup* of the stock and cook, covered, for 15 minutes, checking occasionally for sticking. Add the browned flour and mix until it is completely absorbed (the brown of the flour is no longer visible) and the meat looks moist and very pasty. Add the remaining stock and greens, bring to a boil, reduce the heat to medium, and, occasionally checking the bottom of the pot for sticking, cook until the meat and greens are tender, about 20 minutes. Serve over the rice.

N O T E : Use three kinds of greens for a rounded taste. We often combine spinach, collards, and mustard greens, but experiment and enjoy! You can use beet tops, turnip greens, chard, or any combination of greens, as long as they aren't bitter ones like iceberg lettuce or radicchio.

SEE COLOR PHOTOGRAPH

Chicken-Fried Steak with Pan Gravy

MAKES **4** SERVINGS

Chicken-fried steak is found in diners and truck stops across the country, but with the addition of heavy cream and fresh parsley, we've elevated it to a delicate fork–tender dish.

SEASONING MIX

2½ tablespoons **Chef Paul Prudhomme's Meat Magic**

1 teaspoon ground dried guajillo chile peppers (see page 2)

1 teaspoon ground dried arbol chile peppers (see page 2)

1 teaspoon ground dried New Mexico chile peppers (see page 2)

•

1 pound boneless beef tenderloin steak, filet, or other tender cut of beefsteak, cut into 4 equal portions

¾ cup plus 3 tablespoons all-purpose flour, in all

1 egg

¼ cup milk

2 cups vegetable oil

½ cup chopped onions

1½ cups chicken stock (see page 196)

1 cup heavy cream

2 tablespoons chopped fresh parsley

Combine the seasoning mix ingredients in a small bowl.

Place the meat on a flat surface and pound each steak with a meat mallet or the side of a saucer, turning the meat as you pound it, until about ¼ inch thick. Sprinkle *½ teaspoon* of the seasoning mix on each side of each steak and rub it in well.

Combine *¾ cup* of the flour with *1½ teaspoons* of the seasoning mix in a shallow bowl. Whisk together the egg and milk in another shallow bowl, beating until very frothy and pale yellow.

Heat the oil in a heavy 12-inch skillet over high heat to 350°, about 5 minutes. While the oil is heating, dredge the steaks one at a time in the seasoned flour, then let them soak 1 to 2 minutes in the egg mixture. One at a time, dredge each steak in the flour again, pressing the steak into the flour to coat it thoroughly, and immediately place it in the hot oil. Fry the steak until browned, about 2 to 3 minutes on each side. Remove it from the skillet, set aside and keep warm, and repeat the process with the other 3 steaks. You can fry more than one steak at a time if you can keep track of which one needs to be turned or removed and if you place each steak in the skillet directly after the second dredging in the flour.

Pour into another heavy skillet all but 1 tablespoon of the oil from the skillet in which the steaks were cooked, leaving the residue of juices from the meat and any brown crust remaining on the bottom. Heat over high heat, and when the oil sizzles, add the onions and cook until light golden brown, about 3 minutes. Stir in the remaining 3 tablespoons of flour and gradually add the stock, whisking constantly. Add the remaining seasoning mix and continue whisking until the gravy comes to a boil, about 2 minutes. Add the cream and parsley and cook 1 minute, whisking constantly. Serve immediately.

New England Boiled Dinner

MAKES **6** SERVINGS

Hearty, one-pot dishes such as this one are always welcome on a cold day. They're good for you too, because the cooking liquid forms a gravy that is eaten along with the meat and vegetables, so you're not throwing away the nutrients in the water. I like to serve a little brown mustard or prepared horseradish with this and some freshly made cornbread.

SEASONING MIX 1

2 tablespoons **Chef Paul Prudhomme's Meat Magic**

½ teaspoon ground mace

¼ teaspoon ground nutmeg

•

SEASONING MIX 2

2 tablespoons **Chef Paul Prudhomme's Meat Magic**

1 teaspoon dried dill weed

12 black peppercorns

6 allspice berries

4 cloves

4 small bay leaves

•

1 (4-pound) corned beef brisket, all visible fat removed

8 cups beef stock (see page 198)

1 cup chopped onions

6 cloves garlic, unpeeled

18 small new potatoes

1 medium-size green cabbage, cut into 6 wedges, with a sliver of core left in to hold each wedge together

4½ cups bite-size pieces peeled parsnips

3 cups bite-size pieces peeled rutabagas or turnips (about 2 large or 3 medium-size)

2 small onions, each cut into 8 wedges

6 large carrots, cut in half crosswise and then lengthwise

DAY 1 • Combine the ingredients for seasoning mix 1, sprinkle the mixture over the brisket, and rub it in well. Place the meat in a bowl, cover, and refrigerate overnight.

DAY 2 • Remove the brisket from the refrigerator and let it come to room temperature.

Bring the stock to a boil in a heavy 10-quart pot over high heat. Combine the ingredients for seasoning mix 2 and add the mixture to the pot, along with the chopped onions and the brisket. Bring the stock back to a boil, reduce the heat to low, and simmer, covered, until the meat is tender but not falling apart, about 2 to 2½ hours.

Add the garlic and potatoes and return to a boil. Cover, reduce the heat to low, and simmer for 10 minutes. Return the heat to high and add the cabbage and parsnips, pushing them under the meat. Bring back to a boil, reduce the heat to low, cover, and simmer for 10 minutes. Return the heat to high, add all the remaining vegetables, and push them under the meat. Bring to a boil, reduce the heat to low, cover, and simmer for 5 minutes. Turn off the heat and let sit, covered, for 5 minutes before serving.

Brisket Barbecue

MAKES 8 SERVINGS

When my taste buds say "barbecue," this is the recipe I pull out! You will too, once you taste it. The gravy with this recipe is so tasty that you don't need another sauce, but if you want to take it in a different direction, the Big Bang Barbecue Sauce (page 186) goes great.

SEASONING MIX

3 tablespoons plus 2 teaspoons
  **Chef Paul Prudhomme's Meat
  Magic**
2 teaspoons ground dried guajillo
  chile peppers (see page 2)
2 teaspoons ground dried arbol chile
  peppers (see page 2)
1 teaspoon mustard seeds
½ teaspoon ground coriander

•

1 (4- to 4½-pound) beef brisket
3½ to 4 cups beef stock, in all
  (see page 198)
2 cups chopped onions
1 cup chopped green bell peppers
1½ cups chopped celery
2 cups tomato sauce
5 tablespoons cider vinegar
4 bay leaves
¼ cup packed dark brown sugar
½ cup honey, in all

DAY 1 • Combine the seasoning mix ingredients in a small bowl. Sprinkle 3 tablespoons of the seasoning mix evenly over the brisket and rub it in well. Set aside the remaining seasoning mix. Cover and refrigerate the meat overnight.

DAY 2 • Remove the brisket from the refrigerator and let it come to room temperature.

Preheat the oven to 425°.

Place the brisket in a large roasting pan and roast, uncovered, for 30 minutes. Turn the meat over, add ½ *cup* of the stock, and cook until the meat is fairly tender, checking now and then to be sure it doesn't burn, about 1 hour. If the meat starts to stick hard to the pan, add another ½ *cup* of the stock.

Remove the pan from the oven and reduce the heat to 350°. Remove the meat and place the pan on top of the stove over high heat. Stir in the onions, bell peppers, celery, remaining seasoning mix, tomato sauce, vinegar, bay leaves, and brown sugar. Scrape the bottom of the pan and cook for 6 minutes. Stir in *3 cups* of the stock and ¼ *cup* of the honey, scrape the pan bottom, and bring to a simmer. Return the brisket to the pan and roast, turning the meat once or twice, until tender, about 1 to 1½ hours.

Remove the pan from the oven and place on top of the stove over high heat. Remove the meat and cut it against the grain into thin slices. Return the slices to the gravy in the pan. Reduce the heat and simmer until the meat is very tender and the sauce is thick and dark red-brown, about 45 minutes to 1 hour. Stir in the remaining ¼ cup honey and remove from the heat.

SEE COLOR PHOTOGRAPH

Sunday Roast Beef

When I was growing up, it was a very special occasion to have a piece of beef large enough to roast. We would save it for Sunday, and a Sunday with roast beef was always exciting. Mother had a personal policy of serving each family member's favorite side dish. Mine was candied yams, but dirty rice, mashed potatoes, and black-eyed peas were likely candidates also. The anticipation at the table of seeing the large, caramelized piece of meat emerge out of the wood-burning oven and watching the juices run as it was sliced is a very real memory that still comes to mind when someone says, "Roast beef's for dinner."

3 tablespoons unsalted butter

¾ cup finely diced bell peppers

3 tablespoons plus 1 teaspoon **Chef Paul Prudhomme's Blackened Steak Magic***, in all*

¾ cup finely diced onions

¾ cup finely diced celery

1½ teaspoons minced fresh garlic

1 (3-pound) aged rib-eye roast, about 4 inches thick at thickest part

DAY 1 • Melt the butter over medium heat in a large heavy skillet until half melted. Add the bell peppers and *2 tablespoons* of the Blackened Steak Magic and cook, stirring occasionally, about 3 minutes. Add the onions and celery and cook, stirring occasionally, for 3 minutes. Add the garlic and cook for 1 minute more, stirring and scraping the bottom of the skillet. Remove from the heat and spread the vegetable mixture on a large plate to stop the cooking process and cool.

DONENESS	ROASTING TIME	INTERNAL TEMPERATURE
True rare (a cool red center)	1 hour 20 minutes	127°
Medium-rare	1 hour 40 minutes	138°
Medium	2 hours	148°
Medium-well	2 hours, 20 minutes	158°
Well-done	2 hours, 40 minutes	over 165°

While the vegetable mixture is cooling, trim the roast of all silver skin and the USDA stamp and trim the fat cap to ¼ inch thick. Lay the roast, fat side up, in a roasting pan without a rack. Sprinkle the roast evenly with the remaining Blackened Steak Magic and rub it in well. Spread the bottom of the roast (the side without the fat cap) with ¼ cup of the cooled vegetable mixture, then turn the roast fat side up. Cut 5 or 6 deep slits, about 2 to 3 inches long, lengthwise with the grain into the top of the roast to form pockets, being careful not to cut through to the bottom. Stuff the pockets with vegetable mixture, getting them as full as possible, and spread any remaining mixture on the top and sides of the roast. Cover and refrigerate overnight.

DAY 2 • Preheat the oven to 300°, keeping the roast refrigerated until ready to cook.

Roast, uncovered, to the desired degree of doneness, according to the table above. The use of a meat thermometer is strongly recommended because it is likely to be more accurate than an oven thermostat or even a separate oven thermometer. Cooking time will be less if you start with your roast at room temperature. It will be more or less if the roast is more or less than 4 inches thick.

Remove the roast from the oven and transfer it to a platter or cutting board. Let sit for 15 to 20 minutes before carving.

Eat Your Vegetables

Italian
Vegetarian Casserole

The staff at Magic Seasoning Blends often asks me to create new recipes using our products, and this casserole is a direct result of that request. It's also a good example of how versatile the blends are—we specified Seafood Magic, but don't be afraid to experiment and use Vegetable Magic or any of the other varieties.

8 cups mixed vegetable florets
   (broccoli, cauliflower, and
   broccoflower)
2 (14½-ounce) cans diced tomatoes
1 teaspoon minced fresh garlic
1 tablespoon plus 1 teaspoon **Chef
Paul Prudhomme's Seafood
Magic**

½ cup freshly grated Parmesan
   cheese, preferably imported
1 tablespoon sugar
4 ounces freshly grated mozzarella
   cheese, preferably imported

Preheat the oven to 350°.

Combine the vegetable florets, tomatoes, garlic, Seafood Magic (or other Magic Seasoning), Parmesan cheese, and sugar in a large bowl and toss to mix thoroughly. Transfer to a 9×9-inch baking pan, sprinkle with the mozzarella cheese, and bake for 35 minutes.

Jumbled Greens

Anyone who knows me knows I really like greens. I like them cooked in with meat, and I enjoy them, like this, by themselves with wonderful seasonings. And since we use vegetable stock instead of chicken stock, this dish is perfect for those who abstain from meat products.

2 tablespoons peanut oil

1½ cups chopped onions

1 bunch collard greens, washed, stemmed, and torn into 3- to 4-inch pieces

1 tablespoon plus 1 teaspoon **Chef Paul Prudhomme's Vegetable Magic**

1 bunch mustard greens, washed, stemmed, and torn into 3- to 4-inch pieces

½ cup chopped fresh cilantro

1 cup vegetable stock, in all (see page 195)

1 (10-ounce) bag fresh spinach, washed, stemmed, and torn into 3- to 4-inch pieces

1 teaspoon sugar

Preheat a heavy (preferably cast-iron) 4-quart pot over high heat to 350°, about 4 minutes. Add the oil and, when it begins to smoke, about 4 minutes, add the onions. Cook, stirring occasionally, until the onions begin to turn golden brown, about 6 minutes, then add the collard greens and the Vegetable Magic. Scrape the bottom of the pot and cook, stirring occasionally, until the greens are sticking on the bottom and about to burn, about 3 to 4 minutes. Add the mustard greens and cilantro and stir and cook for 1 minute. Add ½ cup stock and scrape the bottom of the pot. The greens will cook down, and the onions will turn dark brown. Cook until all the liquid evaporates, about 10 to 12 minutes, then add the remaining stock. Scrape the bottom of the pot and add the spinach. Stir and cook for 3 minutes. Add the sugar and cook for 1 minute longer. Remove from the heat and serve.

Baked Stuffed Onions

MAKES **6** TO **8** SIDE-DISH SERVINGS

Almost everyone uses onions as flavoring, but in this recipe we've used them as a side dish. With a delicious meat stuffing that enhances their delicate sweet flavor, they take the spotlight as a beautiful dish in their own right.

SEASONING MIX

5 tablespoons plus 2 teaspoons
   **Chef Paul Prudhomme's Pork
   and Veal Magic**
2 teaspoons dry mustard
1½ teaspoons dried sweet basil
   leaves
1½ teaspoons dried thyme leaves

•

6 large or 8 medium-size onions
½ cup coarsely chopped pecans

4 tablespoons unsalted butter
1¼ cups chopped onions, in all
½ cup chopped green bell peppers
¼ cup chopped celery
½ pound ground lean pork
½ teaspoon minced fresh garlic
¾ cup uncooked converted rice
2 cups chopped fresh mushrooms
2 cups pork or chicken stock, in all
   (see page 198 or 196)
1 (12-ounce) can evaporated milk
2 cups grated Monterey Jack cheese
continued

Combine the seasoning mix ingredients in a small bowl. Reserve *2 table-spoons* of this mixture if you are using 6 onions, or *2 tablespoons plus 2 tea-spoons* for 8 onions.

Peel the onions and cut a thin slice off the top of each so they will stand without tipping. Turn each onion over and scoop out the insides with a melon baller, leaving a shell about ½ inch thick. Cut a very thin slice off each of the 4 sides of each onion to keep them from rolling in the skillet, so they will brown evenly.

Toast the pecans in a dry 10-inch skillet over medium heat, flipping and shaking or stirring them until they are lightly roasted, about 3 minutes. Remove the pecans from the skillet and set them aside.

Wipe the skillet clean, return it to high heat, and add the butter. When the butter sizzles, add the onion cups, laying them on their sides, and cook, turning occasionally, until they are browned on all sides, about 2 minutes. Remove the onion cups and set aside.

To the skillet add ¾ *cup* of the chopped onions and all the peppers and celery and cook until they are browned, about 4 minutes. Add the pork and garlic and cook until browned, breaking up the meat with a spoon, about 3 minutes. Stir in *1 tablespoon* of the seasoning mix and the remaining ½ cup chopped onions and cook for 1 minute. Stir in the rice and the remaining seasoning mix and cook for 3 minutes. Add the mushrooms and cook for 1 minute, scraping as the mixture begins to stick to the bottom of the skillet. Stir in *1¼ cups* stock and cook until it is reduced and the mixture forms a crust on the bottom of the skillet, about 8 minutes. Add the evaporated milk and pecans and scrape the skillet. Bring to a rolling boil, cover, and remove from the heat. Let sit, covered, for 20 minutes.

Preheat the oven to 375°. Sprinkle each onion cup all over with *1 tea-spoon* of the reserved seasoning mix, rubbing the mixture inside and out. Place the onions, open ends up, in a pan just large enough to hold them. Fill them with the pork/rice mixture, heaping it up as much as possible, and sprinkle the grated cheese on top. Pour the remaining ¾ cup stock into the bottom of the pan and bake for 20 minutes. Turn the oven up to 550° and bake another 10 minutes, or until brown and bubbly on top. Serve with a little sauce from the pan spooned over each onion.

Bobby's Sweet Pea Salad

★☆★☆★☆

Growing up on a farm, we always had green peas in our winter garden, and Mom cooked them with a little sugar. My brother Bobby originated this particular recipe—one of many versions we enjoyed. If you can find fresh peas at the market, by all means use them, as the flavor is far superior. Better yet, find a spot in your garden and grow your own. Bobby did.

5 cups water
2¼ pounds unshelled fresh green
    peas (a generous 3 cups shelled)
    plus 1 tablespoon sugar or 1
    (17-ounce) can small sweet peas
1 tablespoon **Chef Paul
    Prudhomme's Magic Pepper
    Sauce**

½ cup Homemade Mayonnaise (see
    page 193)
1 cup finely chopped red onions
2 hard-boiled eggs, peeled and
    chopped
2 tablespoons **Chef Paul
    Prudhomme's Vegetable Magic**

If using fresh peas, bring the water to a boil in a 2-quart saucepan. Add the shelled peas and sugar, cover, and return to a boil. Reduce the heat, remove the lid, and simmer until the peas are tender but still firm, about 11 minutes. Immediately drain the peas in a colander and let cool about 10 minutes.

If using canned peas, they are already cooked, so just drain them well.

In a serving bowl, stir the Magic Pepper Sauce into the mayonnaise and blend thoroughly. Add the peas, onions, chopped eggs, and Vegetable Magic, and mix well. Serve warm or chilled.

Magic Broiled Tomatoes

Quick and easy to make, this dish is a perfect accompaniment to just about any meat, fish, or poultry main course. In Great Britain and Ireland, broiled tomatoes are a standard part of breakfast. Try this recipe in the morning for a real change of pace.

2 medium-size tomatoes, peeled (see page 3)
1 tablespoon plus 1 teaspoon unsalted butter, softened

*2 teaspoons **Chef Paul Prudhomme's Vegetable Magic***
1 tablespoon freshly grated Parmesan cheese, optional

Preheat the broiler.

Slice an "X" into the tops of the tomatoes to about halfway down and set them aside.

Make a paste of the butter, Vegetable Magic, and, if desired, the Parmesan cheese. Spread half of the mixture on top of each tomato, pushing a little of the mixture down into the scoring. Place the tomatoes in a shallow pan, seasoned side up. Broil with the tomato tops about 1 inch from the heat until the tops are brown and crusty, about 3 minutes. Spoon the juices from the bottom of the pan over the tops and serve immediately.

Smothered Cabbage

Sometimes you need something simple and uncomplicated to balance your meal perfectly, and this delicious cabbage might be just the thing. It's great with highly seasoned meats, especially if they're rich and heavy, because although it's very tasty, this dish is light. And easy too.

2 tablespoons olive oil	½ cup chopped celery
2 tablespoons unsalted butter	1 tablespoon plus 2 teaspoons **Chef**
1 head green cabbage, chopped into	**Paul Prudhomme's Vegetable**
1-inch pieces, in all	**Magic**
2 cups chopped onions	1 cup vegetable stock, in all
2 cups chopped green bell peppers	(see page 195)

Preheat a heavy 12-inch skillet or 4-quart pot (preferably cast-iron) to 350°, about 4 to 5 minutes, and add the oil and butter. When the oil begins to smoke, add half the cabbage and the onions, bell peppers, celery, and Vegetable Magic. Cook, stirring occasionally, until the vegetables begin to stick, about 8 to 9 minutes. Add ½ cup of the stock, scrape the bottom of the pot, and add the remaining cabbage. Mix well, cover, and cook, stirring once or twice, until the second addition of cabbage is fork tender, about 7 to 8 minutes. Add the remaining ½ cup of stock only if the liquid in the pot evaporates completely and the cabbage is in danger of scorching.

K-Paul's
Mashed Potatoes

This is the way we make mashed potatoes at K-Paul's, and our customers say they are to die for! Since people are always asking what our secret is, we thought we'd share it with you. If a potato dish can be considered first class, this one definitely is. Some of our regular customers even order it for dessert!

3 medium-size to large potatoes, about 3 pounds, peeled	*2 cups heavy cream*
¼ pound (1 stick) unsalted butter, melted	*2 tablespoons plus ½ teaspoon* **Chef Paul Prudhomme's Vegetable Magic**

Dice 1 potato into 1-inch cubes and the other 2 into ½-inch cubes.

Add enough water to a large pot to measure 1½ inches deep and place over high heat. When the water boils, add the potatoes, cover, and cook until the large-dice potatoes are fork tender, about 20 to 25 minutes. Drain thoroughly.

While the potatoes are draining, melt the butter in a small skillet, then remove from the heat.

Place the drained potatoes in a food processor or mixer and process until smooth (you may have to do this in batches). With the machine running, slowly add the melted butter to the potatoes, and when it is mixed in, add the cream. Process only until the potatoes are stiff but not dry, about 3 to 4 minutes. When the potatoes reach the right consistency, add the Vegetable Magic and pulse a couple of times, just to mix it in.

Corn Pudding

MAKES 6 TO 8 SIDE-DISH SERVINGS

★ ☆ ★ ☆ ★ ☆ ★

Almost everyone—from the earliest Native Americans to present-day folks—loved and loves corn, and this recipe gives you one more way to cook it. Notice that we've used Poultry Magic, even though the recipe contains ham, but you could certainly substitute Pork and Veal Magic. I always hope that you eaters will take my recipes and experiment with them, making each one special and exciting for your own taste buds!

5 tablespoons unsalted butter

1½ cups diced lean ham, about
  6 ounces

1½ cups chopped onions

1 cup chopped green bell peppers

1 tablespoon plus 1 teaspoon **Chef Paul Prudhomme's Poultry Magic**

3 cups fresh corn kernels (about
  6 ears)

½ cup yellow cornmeal

1 cup canned evaporated milk

1½ cups whole milk, in all

4 eggs

Vegetable oil cooking spray

Melt the butter in a 10-inch skillet over high heat. When the butter sizzles, add the ham, onions, and bell peppers. Cook, stirring, until the vegetables are soft, about 4 minutes. Stir in the Poultry Magic and cook, stirring once, until a light crust forms on the bottom of the skillet, about 4 minutes. Add the corn, scrape the bottom of the skillet, and cook 4 minutes. Stir in the cornmeal and cook, scraping the bottom of the skillet to keep the cornmeal from burning, about 1 to 2 minutes. Add the evaporated milk and scrape the bottom of the skillet thoroughly. Add ½ cup of the whole milk,

continued

scrape the bottom of the skillet again, and remove from the heat. Let cool a few minutes.

Preheat the oven to 350°.

Whip the eggs with a whisk in a medium-size bowl until frothy, about 45 seconds. Add the remaining 1 cup whole milk and whip until thoroughly blended. Fold the cooled corn mixture into the egg mixture.

Coat a 9×9-inch baking dish with cooking spray, pour in the corn mixture, and bake until the pudding is set, about 35 to 45 minutes. Cut into wedges or spoon onto plates and serve warm.

Corn Maque Choux

MAKES 10 TO 12 SIDE-DISH SERVINGS

Maque choux, pronounced "mock-shoe," is a traditional south Louisiana dish that always contains corn, but you can also add seafood or diced cooked chicken or ham. It's great served with chopped fresh tomatoes on top.

4 tablespoons unsalted butter
¼ cup vegetable oil
7 cups fresh corn kernels (about 14 ears) or frozen corn kernels
1 cup very finely chopped onions
¼ cup sugar
2 teaspoons **Chef Paul Prudhomme's Vegetable Magic**

2¼ cups chicken, beef, or pork stock, in all (see page 196 or 198)
4 tablespoons margarine
1 cup evaporated milk, in all
2 eggs

In a large skillet, preferably nonstick, combine the butter and oil with the corn, onions, sugar, and Vegetable Magic. Cook over high heat until the corn is tender and a crust starts to form on the bottom of the skillet, about 12 to 14 minutes, stirring occasionally, then stirring more as the mixture starts sticking. Gradually stir in *1 cup* of the stock, scraping the bottom of the skillet to remove the crust as you stir. Continue cooking for 5 minutes, stirring occasionally. Add the margarine, stir until melted, and cook about 5 minutes, stirring frequently and scraping the skillet as needed. Reduce the heat to low and cook about 10 minutes, stirring occasionally, then add ¼ *cup* additional stock and cook about 15 minutes, stirring fairly frequently. Add the remaining 1 cup of stock and cook about 10 minutes, stirring occasionally. Stir in ½ *cup* of the milk and continue cooking until most of the liquid is absorbed, about 5 minutes, stirring occasionally. Remove from the heat.

Combine the eggs and the remaining ½ cup milk in a bowl and beat with a whisk until very frothy, about 1 minute. Add this mixture to the corn, stirring well. The heat from the corn will cook the eggs just enough to give this dish a rich, frothy texture. Serve immediately.

SEE COLOR PHOTOGRAPH

Potatoes au Gratin

MAKES 8 TO 10 SIDE-DISH SERVINGS

You're in for a real treat if your previous experience with potatoes au gratin has been with boxed versions. You'll need a big casserole in which to bake this dish, which is big, rich, and very satisfying.

SEASONING MIX
3 tablespoons plus 2 teaspoons
  Chef Paul Prudhomme's
  Vegetable Magic
2½ teaspoons paprika
½ teaspoon ground nutmeg

•

10 cups sliced peeled potatoes
  (about 7 medium-large, sliced
  ¼ inch thick)
8 tablespoons (1 stick) unsalted
  butter, in all

¾ cup grated onions
2½ cups grated peeled potatoes
2 cups chicken stock, in all
  (see page 196)
½ cup finely diced red bell peppers
¼ cup finely chopped fresh parsley
1 cup milk
1 cup heavy cream
3 cups grated sharp Cheddar
  cheese, in all
1 cup grated Monterey Jack cheese

Combine the seasoning mix ingredients in a small bowl.

Bring a large pot of water to a boil over high heat. Add the sliced potatoes, return to a boil, and cook until just firm-tender, about 2 to 3 minutes. Drain and rinse under cold running water.

Melt *4 tablespoons* of butter in a 12-inch skillet over high heat. When it begins to sizzle, add the onions and cook, stirring occasionally, until they are golden, about 4 to 5 minutes. Stir in *1 tablespoon* of the seasoning mix, the grated potatoes, and the remaining 4 tablespoons butter. Cook about 5 minutes, scraping often with a spatula to keep a crust from forming on the bottom of the skillet. Add *1 tablespoon* of the seasoning mix and *1 cup* of the stock and cook, scraping the bottom of the pan occasionally, until the mixture is thick, light brown in color, and sticking hard to the bottom of the skillet, about 5 to 6 minutes. Add the bell peppers, parsley, remaining 1 cup stock, and remaining seasoning mix and cook, stirring occasionally, for 3 minutes. Whisk in the milk, breaking up the grated potatoes (they will act as a thickening starch). Bring to a rolling boil and cook, whisking occasionally, until the sauce is light brown, about 4 minutes. Add the cream and return to a boil, whisking occasionally. Reduce the heat to low and simmer, whisking occasionally, until very thick, about 4 to 5 minutes. Add *1 cup* of the Cheddar and all the Monterey Jack cheese and cook, whisking, until the sauce returns to a boil. Remove from the heat.

Preheat the oven to 375º.

Pour a thin layer of the sauce over the bottom of a large, deep casserole dish, about 10×10×4 inches. Add the sliced potatoes and pour the remaining sauce over them. Sprinkle the top with the remaining 2 cups of grated Cheddar cheese. Bake, uncovered, until brown and bubbly on top, about 25 minutes.

Southern Smothered Spuds

MAKES 6 TO 8 SIDE-DISH SERVINGS

We eat a lot of potatoes in the South, particularly away from coastal regions, where rice usually predominates. And we like them tender and well seasoned, as these are. One reason this version is so tasty is that we cook the potatoes over high heat and let them form a crust in the bottom of the skillet, a process that brings out all their natural sweetness.

SEASONING MIX

1 tablespoon plus 1 teaspoon **Chef Paul Prudhomme's Meat Magic**
1 teaspoon dried basil leaves
1 teaspoon dried cilantro leaves
¼ teaspoon ground allspice

4 tablespoons unsalted butter
3 medium-size potatoes, peeled and sliced ½ inch thick
3 cups sliced onions
1 cup chicken stock (see page 196)

•

Combine the seasoning mix ingredients in a small bowl.

Melt the butter in a 12-inch skillet over high heat. When it starts to sizzle, stir in the seasoning mix. Add the potatoes, cover, and cook until the potatoes start to turn golden and stick hard to the skillet, occasionally scraping up the crust as it forms on the bottom of the skillet, about 4 to 6 minutes. Add the onions, cover, and cook, occasionally scraping the bottom of the skillet, until the potatoes are sticking hard to the skillet and a golden brown crust has formed, about 6 to 8 minutes. Add the stock, scrape the bottom of the skillet until clean, and cook, uncovered, until the stock is completely absorbed by the potatoes, about 3 to 4 minutes. Remove from the heat, cover, and let sit for 5 minutes before serving.

★

Traditional Potato Salad

MAKES **6** TO **8** SIDE-DISH SERVINGS

You can serve this salad with our Green Onion Salad Dressing (page 192) or with Homemade Mayonnaise (page 193). Either way, it's wonderful.

*2 tablespoons plus 1 teaspoon **Chef Paul Prudhomme's Vegetable Magic***

1 teaspoon salt

1½ cups salad dressing or mayonnaise

4 medium-size white potatoes, cooked, peeled, and diced into ½-inch cubes

6 hard-boiled eggs, peeled and finely chopped

¼ cup finely diced onions

¼ cup finely diced celery

¼ cup finely diced green bell peppers

Blend the Vegetable Magic and salt into the salad dressing or mayonnaise in a large bowl, then add all the remaining ingredients. Mix well and refrigerate until ready to serve.

SEE COLOR PHOTOGRAPH

Hot German Potato Salad

Hot potato salad is a favorite dish in German communities all over the country. It's particularly popular at large gatherings because it keeps well without refrigeration, since there's no mayonnaise in it. It's best served warm but is also good at room temperature and even better a day or two later, after the tart flavor of the vinegar and the sweet tastes of the bacon and sugar have blended completely.

20 unpeeled small red new potatoes
4 hard-boiled eggs, peeled and
  chopped
8 slices bacon, diced
1 cup chopped white onions
2 tablespoons **Chef Paul**
  Prudhomme's Meat Magic

¼ cup all-purpose flour
1 cup chicken stock (page 196)
¾ cup vinegar
½ cup sugar
½ cup chopped green onion tops
  or chives

Cook the potatoes in a large pot of water until tender, about 5 minutes from the time the water starts to boil. Drain and cool under cold running water. Slice the potatoes ¼ inch thick and place them in a large bowl. Add the eggs, mix well, and set aside.

Sauté the bacon in a 10-inch skillet over high heat until browned, about 7 minutes. Remove the bacon from the skillet with a slotted spoon and set aside.

Pour off all but 2 tablespoons of the bacon fat and return the skillet to high heat. Add the onions and cook, scraping the bottom of the skillet occasionally, until the onions are golden, about 3 to 5 minutes. Add the Meat

Magic, then whisk in the flour. Slowly add the stock, vinegar, and sugar, whisking constantly. Cook, whisking frequently, until the mixture is thick, about 5 to 6 minutes. Remove from the heat.

Fold the dressing into the potato and egg mixture, add the green onion tops and cooked bacon, and combine thoroughly.

Candied Yams

MAKES 2 SERVINGS (IF USING FRESH)

Sharp-eyed readers will notice that this recipe doesn't have a grain of Magic Seasoning Blends, but it's included because it's one of my very favorite dishes. If possible, use fresh yams, although the canned variety will still be delicious. If you can't find yams in your community, this recipe works very well with sweet potatoes.

2 medium-size yams, peeled and
   cut into 1½- to 2-inch chunks,
   or 1 (15-ounce) can yams packed
   in syrup (see Note)
1 cup water

¼ cup granulated sugar
¼ cup packed light brown sugar
4 tablespoons unsalted butter, in all
1½ teaspoons vanilla extract
Juice and grated rind from ⅛ lemon

In a 1-quart saucepan, combine the yams, water, sugars, *2 tablespoons* of the butter, the vanilla, and the lemon juice and rind. Cover and cook over
continued

medium heat for 30 minutes, stirring occasionally. Uncover and cook until the yams are fork tender, about 10 minutes. Add the remaining butter and stir until completely melted. Cook, uncovered, until the sauce is thick, about 2 minutes more.

N O T E : To use canned yams, drain them, reserving ½ *cup* of the syrup. In a 1-quart saucepan, place the reserved syrup, ⅓ *cup* granulated sugar, *4 tablespoons* unsalted butter, *1 tablespoon* vanilla extract, and the juice and grated rind from ½ *lemon*. Cook over high heat for 2 minutes, whisking frequently. Add the yams and reduce the heat to very low. Cover and simmer for 10 minutes. Remove the cover and cook until the mixture is reduced to 1 cup, about 10 minutes more, stirring occasionally and being careful not to break up the potato pieces.

SEE COLOR PHOTOGRAPH

Bobby Prudhomme's Macaroni Salad

MAKES 6 TO 8 SIDE-DISH SERVINGS

This recipe was given to me by my brother Bobby, a fellow who was always in motion. From the time he was a little boy, he wanted to be the fastest at everything—eating, working, schoolwork—and this dish is pretty fast to make.

1½ cups Homemade Mayonnaise
   (see page 193)
3 tablespoons **Chef Paul
   Prudhomme's Magic Pepper
   Sauce**
1 tablespoon sugar
1½ teaspoons **Chef Paul
   Prudhomme's Vegetable Magic**
3 cups 1-inch-long shell macaroni,
   about 7 ounces

½ cup plus 2 tablespoons very
   finely chopped red onions
½ cup plus 2 tablespoons very
   finely chopped green bell peppers
3 hard-boiled eggs, peeled and
   chopped

Combine the mayonnaise, Magic Pepper Sauce, sugar, and Vegetable Magic in a large bowl and set aside.

Bring 2 quarts of water to a rapid boil over high heat in a 3-quart saucepan and add the macaroni. Stir well and cook, stirring occasionally, just until tender, about 10 minutes. Immediately drain the macaroni in a colander. Rinse first with hot water to wash off the starch, then rinse well with cold water to stop the cooking. Rinse until cool to the touch and drain well.

Combine the cooled macaroni, onions, peppers, and chopped eggs with the dressing in the bowl and mix thoroughly. Serve immediately or refrigerate and serve well chilled.

SEE COLOR PHOTOGRAPH

Fried Okra
with Red Onions

With only one okra dish in the cookbook, we wanted it to be the best! This dish is excellent served with other fresh summer vegetables, such as corn on the cob, field peas, and sliced garden tomatoes. And be sure to serve plenty of hot buttered cornbread too!

*1 tablespoon plus 1 teaspoon **Chef Paul Prudhomme's Vegetable Magic** or **Chef Paul Prudhomme's Seafood Magic***

½ cup plus 2 tablespoons corn flour (see Note)

½ cup plus 2 tablespoons yellow cornmeal

¾ pound (about 1 quart) untrimmed fresh okra

1 cup packed thinly sliced red onions separated into rings

6 tablespoons vegetable oil

¼ cup white vinegar

½ teaspoon salt, plus a little to sprinkle on the finished okra

½ teaspoon black pepper

Vegetable oil for frying

Combine the Vegetable Magic or Seafood Magic, the corn flour, and the cornmeal in a shallow pan (a pie or cake pan works well) and mix until thoroughly combined. Set aside.

Place the okra in a 2-quart saucepan and cover with water. Bring to a boil over high heat, then continue boiling, stirring occasionally, for 5 minutes. Cover the pan, remove it from the heat, and let sit for 5 minutes. Drain the okra in a colander, then rinse with cool tap water, tossing gently so the okra cools thoroughly while each pod remains intact. Drain well.

Place the okra in a bowl and add the onions, oil, vinegar, ½ teaspoon salt, and black pepper. Mix gently to coat the okra and onion rings well, then let sit for 15 minutes. Drain well and transfer the onions to another bowl. (This drained, seasoned oil and vinegar mixture is good as a salad dressing or to marinate other vegetables for a salad.)

Pour enough fresh vegetable oil in a deep skillet or deep fryer to measure 2 inches deep and heat it to 350°. If you are not using an electric appliance, use a cooking thermometer and adjust the heat to keep the oil temperature at 350°. While the oil is heating, dredge the okra in the seasoned flour mixture, turning with a fork to coat it thoroughly, and let it sit for 5 minutes. Shake off the excess flour and slip the pods into the hot oil one at a time and in a single layer, being careful to keep them intact. Fry in batches without crowding, turning at least once, until very crisp, about 8 minutes. Drain the fried okra on paper towels.

While the last batch of okra is frying, dredge the onions in the same flour mixture, and let them sit for 5 minutes. Fry the onions in batches without crowding in the hot oil until crisp, about 3 minutes, and drain on paper towels. Lightly salt the okra, then toss with the onions and serve immediately.

NOTE: Corn flour is available at health food stores.

Fried Eggplant, Zucchini, or Mirliton

MAKES 1 TO 2 SIDE-DISH SERVINGS

The mirliton, also called vegetable pear or chayote, is grown in the southern part of this country and throughout the warm areas of Latin America. Its vines are so prolific that home gardeners sometimes have trouble giving the vegetables away! With this recipe, you'll be glad to accept their bounty. It makes a great party snack and an unusual appetizer when served with a cheesy dip.

1 cup peeled and diced raw
   eggplant or zucchini, or 1 cup
   peeled and diced cooked mirliton
1 tablespoon **Chef Paul**
   Prudhomme's Vegetable Magic,
   in all

½ cup all-purpose flour
½ cup very fine dry bread crumbs
½ cup milk
1 egg
Vegetable oil for deep-frying
Powdered sugar, optional

Sprinkle the vegetables evenly with *1 teaspoon* of Vegetable Magic, toss gently to distribute, and set aside.

In separate bowls, add *1 teaspoon* of Vegetable Magic to the flour, and *1 teaspoon* to the bread crumbs, and mix each well. In a third small bowl, whisk the milk and egg until well blended.

Pour enough oil to measure 1 inch deep in a 2-quart saucepan, deep-fryer, or large electric skillet and heat it to 350°. When the oil is hot, dredge the vegetables in the seasoned flour and shake off the excess. Work quickly so the flour doesn't pick up too much moisture from the vegetables; it's best to use your hands for this, but a slotted spoon will work too. Then coat the vegetables with the egg/milk mixture and quickly dredge in the bread crumbs, shaking off the excess.

Separate the vegetables as you drop them into the hot oil, and cook them until dark golden brown, about 2 to 3 minutes. (If you're not using an electric appliance, adjust the heat as necessary to keep the oil's temperature about 350°.) Drain on paper towels, and if serving eggplant or zucchini, sprinkle lightly with powdered sugar if desired. Serve immediately.

Succotash

MAKES 6 SIDE-DISH SERVINGS

If you think of succotash as a tired old dish that's been sitting in a cafeteria lineup for 15 hours, then this is the next recipe you should try! You have no idea how wonderful succotash can be until you make it from scratch. Try to use fresh vegetables if possible, but I know fresh lima beans are seldom available, and you may have to use frozen. Any fresh peas or beans or any leftover cooked dried beans such as black-eyed peas, lentils, or chickpeas will certainly make this dish exciting.

continued

4 tablespoons unsalted butter, in all
1½ cups chopped onions
4½ cups fresh corn kernels (about
    8 or 9 ears), in all
1 tablespoon plus 1 teaspoon **Chef
    Paul Prudhomme's Vegetable
    Magic** or **Chef Paul
    Prudhomme's Seafood Magic**,
    in all

2½ cups chicken stock, in all
    (see page 196)
3 cups fresh shelled or frozen lima
    beans
2 cups fresh or frozen green beans,
    cut into 1-inch pieces
1 cup beef stock (see page 198)

Melt *2 tablespoons* butter in a 12-inch skillet over high heat. When it sizzles, add the onions, shake the pan, stir, and cook until the onions start to brown, about 4 minutes. Stir in *2 cups* corn and *2 teaspoons* Vegetable or Seafood Magic and cook until a light crust forms on the bottom of the skillet, about 1 minute. Add ½ *cup* chicken stock and scrape well to remove all the crust from the skillet bottom. Continue to cook without stirring until another hard crust forms on the bottom of the skillet, about 6 to 8 minutes. Add the remaining 2½ cups corn, the lima beans, the remaining Vegetable or Seafood Magic, and another *1 cup* chicken stock. Scrape well, stir, and cook for 2 minutes. Add the green beans, stir, and bring to a simmer, about 2 minutes. Add the remaining 2 tablespoons butter. Stir and cook, flipping and shaking the pan from time to time, for 6 minutes. Stir in the remaining *1 cup* chicken stock and cook, stirring occasionally, for 7 minutes. Add the beef stock, stir, and cook until the lima beans are tender, about 10 minutes.

Sauce Pans and Stock Pots

Tomato Sweet Basil Sauce

MAKES 6 CUPS

★ ☆ ☆ ☆ ☆ ☆

This is the most requested of all our thousands of recipes! Be sure to use fresh basil because dried just doesn't make it. This sauce goes great with either chicken, beef, veal, or seafood or over pasta or rice. Use Seafood Stock and Seafood Magic if you're going to serve it with seafood.

¼ cup olive oil
3 cups finely diced onions
1½ sticks unsalted butter or
   margarine, in all
4 teaspoons minced fresh garlic
3 cups chicken or seafood stock
   (see page 196 or 194)
2 teaspoons Worcestershire sauce

1 tablespoon plus 1 teaspoon **Chef
   Paul Prudhomme's Poultry
   Magic** or **Chef Paul
   Prudhomme's Seafood Magic**
1 tablespoon chopped fresh basil
3 teaspoons light brown sugar
6 cups chopped peeled (see page 3)
   fresh tomatoes

   Heat the olive oil in a 4-quart pot over high heat for 2 minutes. Add the onions and cook, stirring occasionally, until they start to brown, about 3 to 5 minutes. Add ½ *stick* of the butter or margarine and turn the heat to medium. Continue cooking, stirring frequently, until the onions caramelize (turn a rich brown color). Add the garlic and cook for 1 minute. Add the stock, Worcestershire sauce, Poultry (or Seafood) Magic, basil, and sugar. Turn the heat up to medium-high and cook, stirring occasionally, until the mixture is reduced by one fourth, about 6 minutes. Add the tomatoes and cook, stirring occasionally, for 15 to 20 minutes. Reduce the heat, whisk in the remaining butter or margarine, and cook for 2 minutes. The finished sauce should be thick and shiny.

Big Bang Barbecue Sauce

MAKES ABOUT 2 QUARTS

☆☆☆☆☆☆

Generously brush this sauce over the meat when it's almost finished cooking and get ready to taste the fireworks! We didn't name it Big Bang for nothing!

¼ cup (½ stick) margarine
¼ cup vegetable oil
5 tablespoons **Chef Paul Prudhomme's Meat Magic,** in all
5 cups chopped onions, in all
2 cups chopped celery, in all
½ cup freshly squeezed lemon juice
2 cups crushed canned tomatoes
1 cup canned tomato purée
2 tablespoons minced fresh garlic

1¼ cups packed dark brown sugar, in all
1 tablespoon grated fresh lemon peel
½ unpeeled medium orange, cut into quarters
5 cups chicken stock, in all (see page 196)
4 bay leaves
½ cup cider vinegar

Melt the margarine with the oil in a heavy 12-inch skillet over high heat. When it sizzles, stir in *4 tablespoons* of the Meat Magic. Cook, stirring constantly, until the Meat Magic starts to darken, about 1 minute. Add *3 cups* of the onions and *1 cup* of the celery, stir well, and cook for 2 minutes. Cover and cook for 3 minutes, then stir and scrape the pan bottom well. Cover and cook for another 3 minutes, then stir and scrape the pan bottom again. Cover and cook 3½ minutes more; stir and scrape up all the brown bits. Cover again and cook for 3 minutes, then add the lemon juice and deglaze the pan. Scrape the sides and bottom of the pan to get up all the brown bits, and cook, stirring occasionally, for 1 minute.

Add the crushed tomatoes, tomato purée, garlic, ½ *cup* of the brown sugar, and the lemon peel. Cook for 2 minutes, then add the orange quarters and the remaining Meat Magic. Cook, stirring occasionally, for 3 minutes more. Add *2 cups* of the stock, the remaining onions and celery, and the bay leaves. Stir well and cook, stirring occasionally, for 7 minutes. Stir in *1 cup* more stock and bring to a boil, stirring occasionally. Reduce the heat to low and simmer, stirring occasionally, for 30 minutes. Stir in *1 cup* more stock, the remaining brown sugar, and the vinegar. Cook, stirring occasionally, for 40 minutes. Stir in the remaining stock and cook, stirring occasionally, until the sauce thickens somewhat and the flavors blend, about 45 minutes.

SEE COLOR PHOTOGRAPH

★

Mamou Marinara

MAKES 9 OUNCES

This simple-to-make little sauce really zings up pasta, meat loaf, broiled chicken, or grilled fish. It's named for Mamou, a tiny little town near Opelousas in south Louisiana that prides itself on the quality of its cooks.

continued

1 tablespoon unsalted butter

1 cup chopped onions

½ teaspoon chopped fresh basil

1 cup crushed canned tomatoes

¾ teaspoon **Chef Paul Prudhomme's Meat Magic**

¾ teaspoon **Chef Paul Prudhomme's Seafood Magic**

1 teaspoon minced fresh garlic

1 cup chicken stock (see page 196)

1 teaspoon sugar

Preheat an 8-inch skillet over high heat for 2 minutes. Add the butter and onions, and cook until the onions start to clear, about 3 to 4 minutes. Add the basil and cook for 1 to 2 minutes. Add the tomatoes, Magic Seasonings, and garlic and cook for 5 minutes, scraping occasionally to prevent sticking. Add the stock, bring to a boil, reduce the heat, and simmer for 20 minutes. Remove from the heat, add the sugar, and purée.

Magic Pizza Sauce

MAKES ABOUT 1 QUART, OR ENOUGH FOR 4 SMALL PIZZAS

Thanks to Pizza & Pasta Magic—either the Herbal or the Hot & Sweet blend will work beautifully in this recipe—you can whip up a fresh sauce in hardly any time at all. If you don't have time for a real pizza, you can spread some sauce on a slice of French bread and top with grated mozzarella and a sprinkling of Pizza & Pasta Magic. This is also a marvelous sauce for pasta. Because Pizza & Pasta Magic contains no added salt, your taste buds may tell you to sprinkle on a little salt.

1 tablespoon unsalted butter

1½ tablespoons olive oil

1 cup chopped onions

2 tablespoons tomato paste

1 tablespoon minced fresh garlic

1 tablespoon plus 1 teaspoon **Chef Paul Prudhomme's Pizza & Pasta Magic**

½ cup light red wine (we used cabernet sauvignon), in all

1 (16-ounce) can chopped tomatoes

1 (8-ounce) can tomato sauce

1 tablespoon finely diced onions

1 tablespoon plus 1 teaspoon light brown sugar

Melt the butter in the olive oil in a 1-quart saucepan over high heat. When the mixture begins to sizzle, add the chopped onions and cook, stirring frequently, until the onions are golden brown, about 7 minutes. Add the tomato paste, garlic, and Pizza & Pasta Magic. Cook over high heat, stirring occasionally to prevent sticking, until the tomato paste becomes dark red-brown, about 4 minutes. Add ¼ *cup* wine, scrape up any crust that forms, then cook until the wine evaporates and the sauce is thick, pasty, and slightly oily-looking. Add the remaining wine and stir until the mixture is thick and smooth, about 2 minutes. Add the chopped tomatoes, tomato sauce, finely diced onions, and brown sugar. Reduce the heat to medium-low and cook until the sauce is thick and bubbly, about 15 minutes.

Remoulade Sauce

This classic New Orleans sauce is traditionally served over iced boiled shrimp or crabmeat, but it's so delicious you'll probably think of all kinds of good things to have with it. One member of my staff says that he likes it with roast beef.

2 egg yolks

¼ cup vegetable oil

½ cup finely diced celery

½ cup finely diced green onions

¼ cup chopped fresh parsley

¼ cup finely grated fresh or prepared horseradish

¼ lemon, seeded

1 bay leaf, crumbled

2 tablespoons Creole (preferred) or brown mustard

2 tablespoons catsup

2 tablespoons Worcestershire sauce

1 tablespoon prepared mustard

1 tablespoon vinegar

1 tablespoon **Chef Paul Prudhomme's Magic Pepper Sauce**

2 tablespoons **Chef Paul Prudhomme's Vegetable Magic**

1 tablespoon minced fresh garlic

2 teaspoons paprika

Beat the egg yolks in a blender or food processor for 2 minutes. With the machine running, slowly add the oil in a thin stream. Blend in the remaining ingredients, one at a time, until well mixed and the lemon rind is finely chopped. Chill well.

Sherry Wine Sauce

MAKES ABOUT 1 CUP

☆☆☆☆☆☆

When my niece, Brenda, who heads our K-Paul's Catering division, plans a party, she always includes mounds of popcorn shrimp with this sauce on the side for dipping. It works just as well with any kind of fried seafood, and it couldn't be easier to make!

1 egg yolk
¼ cup catsup
3 tablespoons finely chopped green
  onions
2 tablespoons dry sherry
1 teaspoon Creole mustard
  (preferred) or brown mustard

¼ teaspoon salt
¼ teaspoon white pepper
¼ teaspoon **Chef Paul
  Prudhomme's Magic Pepper
  Sauce**
½ cup vegetable oil

Place all the ingredients except the oil in a food processor or blender and process for 30 seconds. With the machine still running, add the oil in a thin, steady stream. Continue processing until smooth, about 1 minute, stopping and pushing the sides down once with a rubber spatula.

Green Onion Salad Dressing

MAKES ABOUT 1½ CUPS

I created this dressing many years ago, and it goes great with potato salad, a fresh green salad, and especially a huge plate of sliced cucumbers. It's also a marvelous dipping sauce for raw vegetables.

1 egg plus 1 egg yolk
1⅛ cups vegetable oil
Scant ½ cup finely diced green
　onions
1½ tablespoons Creole (preferred)
　or brown mustard

1 tablespoon vinegar
1 teaspoon **Chef Paul
　Prudhomme's Vegetable Magic**

Whip the egg and egg yolk in a food processor or blender until frothy, about 2 minutes. With the machine on, gradually add the oil in a thin stream. When the mixture is thick and creamy, add the remaining ingredients and blend thoroughly. Refrigerate until ready to use.

Homemade Mayonnaise

We've all eaten store-bought mayonnaise, but if you haven't had fresh homemade mayonnaise lately, you have to try this. It'll make a hamburger richer and a hot dog tastier. You'll even appreciate the end of your finger if you dip it in there and lick it.

1 large egg
¼ cup vegetable oil
1 tablespoon cider vinegar
1 teaspoon **Chef Paul Prudhomme's Magic Pepper Sauce**

½ teaspoon black pepper
½ teaspoon white pepper

Place the egg in a blender and process for 30 seconds. With the machine running, slowly add the oil in a thin, steady stream. Add the vinegar and process for 30 seconds. Add the Magic Pepper Sauce and the black and white peppers and process just until blended.

Seafood Stock

If you're used to making seafood dishes with plain water, you're going to be pleased with how much richer and more flavorful they are when you use stock.

2 quarts cool tap water
Vegetable trimmings from recipe
  you're cooking, if available
1 medium-size onion, unpeeled and
  quartered
1 rib celery with leafy top,
  quartered

1 large clove garlic, unpeeled and
  quartered
Shells from shrimp or crawfish, or
  scraps from fish in recipe you're
  cooking (see Note)

Place all the ingredients in a large stockpot over high heat and bring to a boil. Reduce the heat and simmer, adding water only if the liquid falls below 1 quart. Cook the stock for 4 hours if possible or as long as you can—even stock simmered for as little as 30 minutes is better than water.

Strain through several layers of cheesecloth before using. The recipe can be doubled or tripled if your stockpot is big enough. You can keep leftover stock for several days in the refrigerator or freeze it for future use.

If you reduce your stock, it will take up even less storage space. To reduce stock, after straining it, pour it into a clean stockpot and bring it back to a boil over high heat. As soon as it boils, lower the heat and simmer the stock until it is reduced to the desired level. After cooling, refrigerate or freeze. This produces a very rich stock that can be used as is or, if you don't want stock with so concentrated a flavor, diluted before use.

Label any container of stock that is to be refrigerated or frozen with the date and the type of stock.

NOTE: If you need to use the shells in the recipe itself (as in Barbecued Shrimp) or if the fish recipe calls for fillets, just buy a little extra for the stock.

★

Vegetable Stock

MAKES 1 QUART

You can make stock in any pot that is large enough to hold all the ingredients, but it's easiest in a stockpot, which is taller than it is wide. This shape means the liquid will have less surface in proportion to its volume than it does in a wider pot, so will evaporate more slowly, yet the stock will cook well and the flavors will be nicely concentrated. In addition to the vegetables mentioned below, you can use just about any you have on hand except bell peppers, which would make the stock spoil faster. And never add salt, herbs, or spices to stock.

2 quarts cool tap water
Vegetable trimmings from recipe
  you're cooking, if available
1 medium-size onion, unpeeled and
  quartered

1 rib celery with leafy top,
  quartered
1 large clove garlic, unpeeled and
  quartered

continued

Place all the ingredients in a large stockpot over high heat and bring to a boil. Reduce the heat and simmer, adding water only if the liquid falls below 1 quart. Cook the stock for 4 hours if possible or as long as you can—even stock simmered for as little as 30 minutes is better than water.

Strain through several layers of cheesecloth before using. The recipe can be doubled or tripled if your stockpot is big enough. You can keep leftover stock for several days in the refrigerator or freeze it for future use.

If you reduce your stock, it will take up even less storage space. To reduce stock, after straining it, pour it into a clean stockpot and bring it back to a boil over high heat. As soon as it boils, lower the heat and simmer the stock until it is reduced to the desired level. After cooling, refrigerate or freeze. This produces a very rich stock that can be used as is or, if you don't want stock with so concentrated a flavor, diluted before use.

Label any container of stock that is to be refrigerated or frozen with the date and the type of stock.

Chicken Stock

MAKES 1 QUART

Chicken stock is incredibly versatile. Not only is it a necessity for most of my chicken dishes, but it is great for cooking other things, such as rice and pasta, making them more delicious than you might have imagined. You can also use it as a substitute for any other stock in an emergency.

2 quarts cool tap water

Vegetable trimmings from recipe
  you're cooking, if available

1 medium-size onion, unpeeled and
  quartered

1 rib celery with leafy top,
  quartered

1 large clove garlic, unpeeled and
  quartered

Back, neck, and giblets (except
  liver) from chicken you're cooking
  (or buy chicken wings or other
  inexpensive parts)

Place all the ingredients in a large stockpot over high heat and bring to a boil. Reduce the heat and simmer, adding water only if the liquid falls below 1 quart. Cook the stock for 4 hours if possible or as long as you can—even stock simmered for as little as 30 minutes is better than water.

Strain through several layers of cheesecloth before using. The recipe can be doubled or tripled if your stockpot is big enough. You can keep leftover stock for several days in the refrigerator or freeze it for future use.

To make your stock even richer, first roast the chicken pieces in a 350° oven for 20 to 30 minutes, depending on the size.

If you reduce your stock, it will take up even less storage space. To reduce stock, after straining it, pour it into a clean stockpot and bring it back to a boil over high heat. As soon as it boils, lower the heat and simmer the stock until it is reduced to the desired level. After cooling, refrigerate or freeze. This produces a very rich stock that can be used as is or, if you don't want stock with so concentrated a flavor, diluted before use.

Label any container of stock that is to be refrigerated or frozen with the date and the type of stock.

Beef or Pork Stock

Many of my recipes call for meat stock because the results will be much more delicious than if they're cooked with water. Making stock is easy to do and well worth the little bit of effort. Just get the stock simmering as long before starting to cook as possible, so the flavors will have time to blend well.

2 quarts cool tap water
Vegetable trimmings from recipe
   you're cooking, if available
1 medium-size onion, unpeeled and
   quartered
1 rib celery with leafy top,
   quartered

1 large clove garlic, unpeeled and
   quartered
Bones and scraps from recipe, or ½
   pound soup meat and bone

Place all the ingredients in a large stockpot over high heat and bring to a boil. Reduce the heat and simmer, adding water only if the liquid falls below 1 quart. Cook the stock for 4 hours if possible or as long as you can—even stock simmered for as little as 30 minutes is better than water.

Strain through several layers of cheesecloth before using. The recipe can be doubled or tripled if your stockpot is big enough. You can keep leftover stock for several days in the refrigerator or freeze it for future use.

For an even richer taste, before starting the stock, roast the bones and meat in a 350° oven for 30 minutes, turning once.

If you reduce your stock, it will take up even less storage space. To reduce stock, after straining it, pour it into a clean stockpot and bring it back to a boil over high heat. As soon as it boils, lower the heat and simmer the stock until it is reduced to the desired level. After cooling, refrigerate or freeze. This produces a very rich stock that can be used as is or, if you don't want stock with so concentrated a flavor, diluted before use.

Label any container of stock that is to be refrigerated or frozen with the date and the type of stock.

Index

egg(s):
    Bobby Prudhomme's macaroni salad,
        176–177
    Bobby's sweet pea salad, 163
    eye-opener omelet, 32–33
    foo yung, 36–37
    hot German potato salad, 174–175
    sweet potato omelet, 34–35
    traditional potato salad, 173
egg noodles:
    chicken fricassee, 103–104
    chicken paprika, 118–119
eggplant, fried, 180–181
eye-opener omelet, 32–33

fajitas, beef, 144–145
fettucini and panéed veal, 138–139
fish:
    blackening of, 59–60
    broiled flounder, 82
    bronzed, 67–68
    bronzing of, 60–61
    fry, Friday night, 83
    magic grilled, 87–88
    Napa Valley, 86–87
    oven-fried catfish, 84–85
    seafood gumbo with smoked sausage,
        22–23
    stock, 2, 194–195
flank and greens, 146–147
flounder:
    broiled, 82
    Friday night fish fry, 83
flour, browning, 3
Friday night fish fry, 83
fruit marinade, 110–111
fry-bread, Indian, 130, 131

garlic:
    baked stuffed onions, 161–162
    pasta, fresh, 47
    shrimp and oysters on pasta, 72–73
German potato salad, hot, 174–175
gingersnap gravy, roasted pork with,
        132–133
golden tile fish, magic grilled, 87–88

gravy:
    cream, fried green tomatoes with, 30–31
    gingersnap, roasted pork with, 132–133
    pan, chicken-fried steak with, 148–149
green chili, 20–21
green onion salad dressing, 192
greens:
    and flank, 146–147
    jumbled, 160–161
grouper, in Friday night fish fry, 83
gumbo:
    chicken and smoked sausage, 24–25
    seafood, with smoked sausage, 22–23

ham:
    Basque chicken and shrimp in wine,
        114–115
    chicken and seafood jambalaya, 39–40
    chicken and tasso jambalaya, 37–38
    lentils and rice, 48
    Monday red beans, 53–54
    pasta primavera, 49
    sweet potato omelet, 34–35
    tasso, 3
hash, red flannel, 29
homemade mayonnaise, 193
honey chicken wings, broiled, 93–94
hot and sweet turkey, 123–124

Indian fry-bread, 130–131
Italian vegetarian casserole, 159

jambalaya, chicken:
    and seafood, 39–40
    and tasso, 37–38
julienne, use of term, 4
jumbled greens, 160–161

K-Paul's mashed potatoes, 166

lamb:
    blackening and bronzing table for, 60
    Navajo tacos, 127–129
lentils and rice, 48
lotsa crab crab cakes, 78–79
Louisiana chicken and dumplings,
        98–100

macaroni:
   beef vegetable soup, 9–10
   salad, Bobby Prudhomme's, 176–177
Mamou marinara, 187–188
maque choux, corn, 168–169
marinade, fruit, 110–111
mashed potatoes, K-Paul's, 166
mayonnaise, homemade, 193
meat:
   beef vegetable soup, 9–10
   blackened steak, 64–65
   blackening of, 59–60
   brisket barbecue, 152–153
   bronzing of, 60–61
   chicken-fried steak with pan gravy,
      148–149
   doneness of, 155
   fajitas, beef, 144–145
   flank and greens, 146–147
   loaf, Chef Paul's, 140–141
   Navajo tacos, 127–129
   New England boiled dinner, 150–151
   panéed veal and fettucini, 138–139
   really rich beef and mushrooms,
      142–143
   scalloping of, 3–4
   shepherd's pie, 41–42
   stock, 2, 198–199
   Sunday roast beef, 154–155
   see also pork
Milwaukee potato soup, 14–15
mirliton, fried, 180–181
mole sauce, 107
   tostadas, chicken, 105–107
Monday red beans, 53–54
mushrooms:
   baked stuffed onions, 161–162
   and beef, really rich, 142–143
   chickpeas, and chicken, 55–56
mustard greens:
   and flank, 146–147
   jumbled greens, 160–161

Napa Valley fish, 86–87
Navajo tacos, 127–129
New England boiled dinner, 150–151

noodles:
   chicken fricassee, 103–104
   chicken paprika, 118–119
   really rich beef and mushrooms, 142–143
   see also pasta

okra with red onions, fried, 178–179
omelet:
   egg foo yung, 36–37
   eye-opener, 32–33
   sweet potato, 34–35
onion(s):
   baked stuffed, 161–162
   fried okra with red, 178–179
   salad dressing, green, 192
orange roughy:
   bronzed fish, 67
   Friday night fish fry, 83
oysters:
   chicken and seafood jambalaya, 39–40
   and garlic shrimp on pasta, 72–73
   seafood gumbo with smoked sausage,
      22–23

pan gravy, chicken-fried steak with, 148–149
paprika, chicken, 118–119
pasta:
   beef vegetable soup, 9–10
   Bobby Prudhomme's macaroni salad,
      176–177
   fresh garlic, 47
   garlic shrimp and oysters on, 72–73
   magic chicken, 91
   panéed veal and fettucini, 138–139
   primavera, 49
   San Francisco rice, 46–47
   see also noodles
pea salad, Bobby's sweet, 165
pecans:
   baked stuffed onions, 161–162
   pork curry, 134–135
pepper(s), chile, 2–3
   black bean soup, 16–17
   and cheese chicken, hot, 116–118
   green chili, 20–21
   La Jolla tamale pie, 130–131
   Navajo tacos, 127–129

sweet pea salad, Bobby's, 163
sweet potato(es):
    candied yams, 175–176
    omelet, 34–35

tacos, Navajo, 127–129
talapia:
    bronzed fish, 67
    Napa Valley fish, 86–87
tamale pie, La Jolla, 130–131
tasso, 3
    chicken and seafood jambalaya, 39–40
    and chicken jambalaya, 37–38
    lentils and rice, 48
    sweet potato omelet, 34–35
tilefish, magic grilled, 87–88
tomato(es):
    big bang barbecue sauce, 186–187
    brisket barbecue, 152–153
    chicken and seafood jambalaya, 39–40
    chicken and tasso jambalaya, 37–38
    chicken cacciatore, 112–113
    eye-opener omelet, 32–33
    fried green, with cream gravy, 30–31
    hot and sweet turkey, 123–124
    Italian vegetarian casserole, 159
    magic broiled, 164
    magic pizza sauce, 188–189
    Navajo tacos, 127–129
    peeling of, 3
    soup, cream of, 10–11
    Spanish rice, 45
    sweet basil sauce, 185
    tropical chicken, 110–111
tortillas:
    beef fajitas, 144–145
    chicken mole tostadas, 105–107
    green chili, 20–21
totally veggie vegetarian soup, 18–19
traditional potato salad, 173
tropical chicken, 110–111

trout:
    bronzed fish, 67
    Friday night fish fry, 83
tuna:
    bronzed fish, 67
    magic grilled fish, 87–88
    Napa Valley fish, 86–87
turkey:
    hot and sweet, 123–124
    rex, 121–122
    rice and cheese casserole, 50–51
turnip greens and flank, 146–147

veal:
    blackening and bronzing table for, 60
    and fettucini, panéed, 138–139
vegetables(s):
    Italian vegetarian casserole, 159
    New England boiled dinner, 150–151
    pasta primavera, 49
    shepherd's pie, 41–42
    soup, beef, 9–10
    stock, 1–2, 195–196
    totally veggie vegetarian soup, 18–19
    see also specific vegetables

walleyed pike, magic grilled, 87–88
wine:
    Basque chicken and shrimp in, 114–115
    sauce, sherry, 191
wings, chicken:
    broiled honey, 93–94
    Buffalo, 92–93

yams, candied, 175–176
yellow squash, in sweet potato omelet, 34–35

zucchini:
    fried, 180–181
    sweet potato omelet, 34–35